THE COMPLETE
TRAINING COURSE
FOR
ALTAR GUILDS

THE COMPLETE TRAINING COURSE FOR ALTAR GUILDS

B. DON TAYLOR

MOREHOUSE PUBLISHING

An imprint of Church Publishing Incorporated
Harrisburg—New York

Morehouse Publishing

Morehouse Publishing is an imprint of Church Publishing Incorporated

4775 Linglestown Road

Harrisburg, PA 17112

Cover design by Rick Snizik

Library of Congress Cataloging-in-Publication Data

Taylor, B. Don.
  The complete training course for altar guilds / B. Don Talylor
    p. cm
  ISBN 10 : 0-0-8192-1593-7 (pbk.)
  ISBN 13 : 978-0-8192-1593-2 (pbk.)
  1. Altar guilds—Episcopal Church. 2. Episcopal church—Liturgy
3. Anglican Communion— Liturgy. I. Title
BX 5948.T39   92-40960
247′.08′823—dc20   CIP

Printed in the United States of America

Eighth Printing, 2007

*Dedicated to the memory of
the Venerable David E. Parker*

TABLE OF CONTENTS

TABLE OF CONTENTS (Continued)

TABLE OF CONTENTS (Continued)

TABLE OF CONTENTS (Continued)

TABLE OF CONTENTS (Continued)

TABLE OF CONTENTS

TABLE OF FIGURES (Continued)

TABLE OF FIGURES (Continued)

Figures

TABLE OF EXERCISES

PREFACE

In the history of the Christian church, it was not uncommon for most, if not all, of a congregation to be illiterate. Much of the church ornamentation that we now think of as "art" originated as a means to remind parishioners of Bible stories, events in the life of Christ, and the church. By walking around a cathedral, they could "read" the various stories depicted in carved frescoes of stone and wood, or portrayed on canvas, in mosaics, and with stained glass.

For the same reason, during the medieval period it was common for dramas, or plays, to be performed in the church. These were called *mystery plays* because the subject matter was about the holy mysteries of the faith. They were written to be performed in cycles covering a variety of themes from both the Old and New Testaments. Performances were usually done in conjunction with the Feast of Corpus Christi, beginning in the thirteenth century and continuing as a vital part of worship until the fifteenth century.

In this same tradition, though no longer for the same reasons, passion plays are frequently done either in a parish church or in an elaborate production in an open field or amphitheater, as a part of the Easter celebration. The term *passion* , comes from the Latin word *passio* meaning 'suffering, emotion,' and refers to the suffering of Jesus during his crucifixion.

The main theme of this training program is that every time we celebrate the Eucharist in our parish, we are performing a miniature version of a passion play. If you can accept that concept, then it is easy to picture the role of the altar guild as stagehands, wardrobe personnel, set designers, and, in the words of the King of Siam, "etcetera, etcetera, etcetera."

The efforts to assemble the information contained in this course required two years of loving labor. Major contributions to the theological content were made by the Venerable David E. Parker, retired Archdeacon of the Diocese of Dallas. One month prior to the training manual's completion, Fr. Parker died suddenly in the West Indies, where he was working in an Anglican parish in Dominica. Without his early efforts, this course could never have been completed.

Marjorie Jordan, former altar guild director at St. Luke's Church, Los Gatos, California, is due our gratitude for commissioning the project and constantly supporting us during its production. Special appreciation is due the ladies and gentlemen of the altar guild at St. Luke's for their great assistance in "proving" the content of these pages.

MODULE 1
INTRODUCTION TO COURSE

*Any applicant for work backstage in a theater needs to know
what play is currently being performed. In this case, the "play" is
the same passion play that has been playing for 2000 years.
This module lays the groundwork for your study of the backstage
work you will be doing before, after, and during the passion play.*

TIME:
Approximately 15 minutes

OBJECTIVE:
Given the contents of Module 1, you will be able to demonstrate an understanding of how the altar guild training course is structured by identifying the six major course related terms within 10 minutes, with 100% accuracy. You will be able to identify:
- Module
- Self-Paced
- Flow Charts
- Progress Check
- Resource Material
- Exercises

ACTIVITIES:
- Read the text
- Complete Progress Check

MATERIAL REQUIRED:
- This Module
- Pen or Pencil
- Progress Check

OTHER RESOURCE MATERIAL:
None

COURSE FLOW-CHART

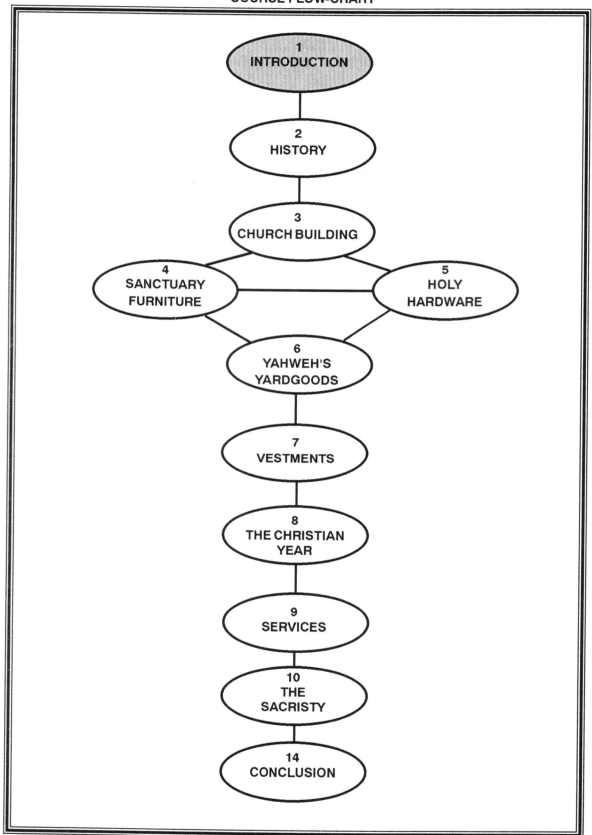

MODULE 1
YOU CAN'T TELL THE PLAYERS WITHOUT A PROGRAM

All too often people feel that anything to do with the Church is shrouded in "holy mystery" that "passeth human understanding." Tragically, they may also feel that their own lack of information or knowledge of terminology somehow makes them less Christian than those who so glibly spout ecclesiastical terms. The simple fact of the matter is that it is just **not** so.

If you fall into either category, take heart. People are not born with their knowledge or vocabulary. They learned it over a period of time. And so can you – except it won't take that long. That's one purpose of this training program. There's nothing mysterious about it. Everything done in the sacristy is done for a perfectly straightforward reason.

Since no one likes to read a training manual (it's boring!), we have attempted to have "fun" with a topic that sometimes can seem tedious – the work of an altar Guild – by comparing the duties and responsibilities to similar activities in a theater. We have made attempts at humor to make the training information more entertaining to read – and because we need to be able to laugh at ourselves. The Lord surely has a sense of humor, otherwise why would he have allowed some of the funny customs that we have adopted in our churches?

Keep in mind that procedures given in this course are in keeping with the traditions of the American Episcopal Church, but many variations occur in actual practice. This study course is written as a *guide* for altar guild members, to unite them in common usage and practice – and not to provide a new "gospel." A key fact to remember as you go through this training program is that regardless of what this (or any other book) says, your rector or vicar is the final authority when it comes to making decisions about liturgical practices in your parish.

After you have completed the training course, you can retain the materials as a handy reference in the future. Now, if we can direct your attention to the "Course Map" on the preceding page, let us tell you how the program is organized.

MODULES
To make the course easier to digest, it has been divided into small portions of information called "modules." This has been done to permit you to pace yourself at a rate that is comfortable for you. A module is simply a logical division of the information.

The only rule is that you finish and understand one unit before moving on to the next. Having mastered the information in one unit, you are ready, able, even anxious to go prayerfully on to the next. The idea is similar to a Thanksgiving feast: if you try to eat everything all at once you're certain to get indigestion. By pacing yourself, you enjoy and savor it more!

Now, about that course map: It is not necessary that you complete the modules in sequence. They are simply presented in an order that seems logical to us, but may not appear logical to you at all. So, any time you complete a module that "branches" to more than one following module, you can choose to complete the "branched" modules in whatever order you wish.

OBJECTIVES

The first page of each module provides an "objective." The objective simply states what you should know by the end of the module. The activities for the module are also listed on the first page, as are the materials that will be needed and any additional resources that may be required.

RESOURCE MATERIAL

Resource material is any additional outside information source that is available. Outside resources are vital, especially in a course about Episcopal Church guilds. Regardless of our level of expertise, on occasion all of us need to use an outside source.

The Book of Common Prayer (BCP) and the Book of Occasional Services are certainly the key resources for any study of holy housework. However, it is a good idea to also make use of other resources, including this training manual and the training aids included with this course.

In addition to the BCP, several readily available resource materials will be used during the course. A quick glance at the first page of each module will tell you whether or not any additional resource material is needed for a particular module.

EXERCISES

Some modules lend themselves to practical exercises to reinforce the information. During these modules, worksheets will be provided, so that you will have all of the material needed to complete your task.

MODULE SUMMARIES

Any good training course should: 1) tell you what you are going to be told (the *objective*), 2) tell you (the *module*), and 3) tell you what you have been told (the *summary*).

At the end of each module you will find a brief summary of the module's main points. It is provided to "jog" your memory about key information.

PROGRESS CHECKS

The progress check is simply a way for you to assure yourself that you have a grasp of the material within the module. This is *not* a test. There are no "trick" questions (or answers) and no one will "grade" your responses – except you. The important thing is for you to feel assured that you know the information, or at least know where to find the information.

If you do not feel confident that you understand some of the points, read the module again. Proceed to the next module when you do feel confident.

ANSWER SHEETS

Following the progress check in each module, you will find answer sheets that allow you to check your responses to any exercises contained in the module, as well as the answers to the progress check.

SUMMARY

In this module you have been introduced to the concept of a self-paced, modularized altar guild training program. You have covered the fact that the information in the course is divided into manageable portions, called modules. Since each module is self-contained, you have the option of following the order of the manual or covering some modules in a different sequence. The course flow chart at the beginning of this module (Module 1) provides a logical sequence and the options available, and can be referred to throughout the course.

The first page of each module provides information on the objective for the module, the activities involved, the materials required and any resource materials. At the end of each module is a summary of the module's content and a progress check.

The progress check is designed to assure you that you have a grasp of the key points of the module. So, if you feel comfortable with the information contained in Module 1, please complete the progress check.

PANIC
THEE
NOT,

COOLETH
IT.

MODULE 1
PROGRESS CHECK

Match the items in column 1 to the appropriate definition in column 2 by inserting the answer in the blank preceding the column 1 items.

_____   **EXERCISES**

_____   **MODULE**

_____   **PROGRESS CHECK**

_____   **SELF-PACED**

_____   **FLOW CHARTS**

_____   **RESOURCE MATERIAL**

A. Indicators of required logical sequence or optional sequence.

B. Additional information other than the material provided in the text of the course.

C. Allows you to spend as much time as needed to feel comfortable with the material.

D. A self-contained, manageable portion of information.

E. A self-test.

F. Helps make a silk purse of a sow's ear.

G. Practice in applying subject material.

(ANSWER SHEET ON BACK OF THIS PAGE)

MODULE 1
ANSWER SHEET

Match the items in column 1 to the appropriate definition in column 2 by inserting the answer in the blank preceding the column 1 items.

__G__ EXERCISES

__D__ MODULE

__E__ PROGRESS CHECK

__C__ SELF-PACED

__A__ FLOW CHARTS

__B__ RESOURCE MATERIAL

If you feel comfortable with your answers, continue to the next module. If not, feel free to review the information in this module.

Hopefully, the marquee some have mentally erected over the sacristy's "stagedoor" proclaiming that the current show is *Abandon Hope All Ye Who Enter Here*, will be replaced with: **Now Showing: *The Episcopal Church Welcomes You*.**

So, let the show begin!

MODULE 2
HISTORY OF ALTAR GUILDS
OR
WHEREFORE AND FROM WHENCE THE ALTAR GUILD

If you're going to work backstage, you need to know the history of your profession. Without the backstage crew the "show" could go on – but the set wouldn't look as nice and the props might be in the wrong place.

TIME:
Approximately 20 minutes

OBJECTIVE:
Given the contents of Module 2, you will be able to demonstrate an understanding of: (1) the history of altar guilds, (2) where they came from and why, and (3) who is qualified for membership in an altar guild by responding to simple fill-in-the blank questions within 10 minutes, with 100% accuracy.

ACTIVITIES:
• Read the text of the module
• Complete Progress Check

MATERIAL REQUIRED:
• This Module
• Pen or Pencil
• Progress Check

OTHER RESOURCE MATERIAL:
None

COURSE MAP

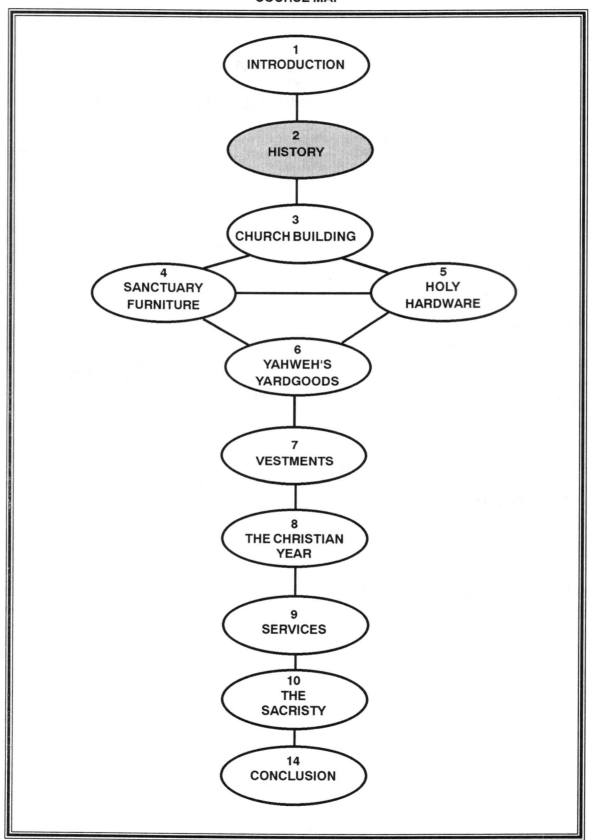

MODULE 2
WHEREFORE AND FROM WHENCE THE ALTAR GUILD

INTRODUCTION

A delightful white-haired lady once enjoyed teasing people who asked her age by saying, "My dear, I won't tell you how old I am, but I was a waitress at the Last Supper." Well, whether true or not, someone had to clean and prepare the room and meal for Jesus and his disciples; and someone had to clean up the room and do the dishes after the whole group departed for the Garden of Gethsemane. We don't think of that person as the founder of altar guilds – though maybe we should.

What are these strange and wonderful things called *altar guilds*? Where did they come from? And, why does the church need them?

A LITTLE HISTORY LESSON

Altar Guilds are a relatively new ministry for lay people, dating only from the last half of the nineteenth century. However, their roots can be traced in antiquity to the very earliest times in the history of the church.

Written around A.D. 200 in Rome, the *Apostolic Tradition* of Hippolytus assigns the care of the vessels to the *subdeacon* , books to the *lector* , and the building to the *doorkeeper* . A little later, there was a person called a *sacristan* whose job was to care for the church building and everything in it. These were some of the "minor orders" of monks or laymen in the church. These minor orders were not observed in the Church of England after the Reformation, so the duties of the sacristan were assumed by the *parish clerk* (among his other responsibilities).

The Oxford and Cambridge movements in the nineteenth-century, stressed increased involvement of the laity in all phases of the church's life, including liturgical ministries. This ended the need for the parish clerk to continue his duties and functions insofar as liturgies and matters dealing with the altar were concerned. Those duties were assumed, for the most part, by a group of women volunteers who (surprise!) became known as the *altar guild.*

QUALIFICATION FOR MEMBERSHIP

Those early members of the nineteenth-century Altar Guild tended to be matronly or maiden ladies of excellent repute, who were not employed outside the home nor raising families. They looked upon their work as a sacred trust, which, indeed it was (and is). But in their fervent zeal, they often made their work seem of such an esoteric, pious nature, they frightened away many younger women, except those possessed of extraordinary dogged determination. (Contrary to what you may think, to our knowledge none of these pious pioneers are currently active members of the altar guild in any American Episcopal parish – not even yours!)

However, in some parishes back then, it seemed that one must wait for one of the "Holy Women" to be called to that "Great Altar Guild in the Sky" before one could hope for an invitation to become a member. (This is not to make fun of the devoted, tireless work of those splendid saints of the sacristy.)

It is sad, but true, that to this day the accumulation of myth, parish custom, legend, and other "unwritten laws" in some parishes can make a new member feel that he or she has become involved in some secret society. In some cases all that seems lacking is a blood oath and a secret handshake!

Altar Guilds Are Still Evolving

As we approach the twenty-first century, the nature of our world requires that some of the stereotypes that we have previously had must now change. It is no longer practical to assume that altar guild members have no other responsibilities outside the church and home. Nor can we take for granted that all members can be on call twenty-four hours a day, seven days a week. This fact does not – and should not – imply that anything less is an indication of reduced dedication on the part of members who must "sandwich" their altar guild service between a host of other activities.

Many of today's altar guild candidates come from the ranks of working parents of school-aged children, who may only be able to devote a few hours once or twice a month. This "new breed" of altar guild membership does require greater organization, better training, and more dependable scheduling.

- *Better organization* in that members need to know what must be done and the most efficient way to do it;
- *Better training* to avoid delays while they wait for someone else to tell them what to do – or wander around attempting to identify a vessel or piece of furniture that they don't know by name; and,
- *Dependable scheduling* that members can "work around" in their private lives and work schedules.

The Sexless Sacristy

As we have stated, altar guilds in the 1800s were composed entirely of women. However, from the beginning men have been used, from time to time, to lift heavy items, climb tall ladders and, in general, "manhandle" items considered too heavy or unseemly for dignified "ladies." In today's altar guild men are now being included in the regular service duty roster. Men can perform the work in the sacristy with as much interest, devotion, and dedication; therefore, guild membership should be open to both sexes. Thus proving the old adage: *"Everything that goes around, comes around,"* – since sacristans/altar guilds were originally monks or laymen in minor orders.

THE PRIEST AND THE ALTAR GUILD

We really had to spend some time on the title of this subsection. Should it be *"The Priest versus the Altar Guild,"* as some parishes seem to play the game? Or should the section be called, *"The Priest and the Altar Guild: God's Team in the Sanctuary?"*

Anyone familiar with the services and liturgies of the church knows why altar guilds are a necessity. The priest cannot begin to do all that must be done in preparation for a service, even if he or she knew how. Seminaries rarely, if ever, teach it. Therefore, the purpose of the altar guild is to assist the clergy. In many places, membership in the altar guild comes through invitation by the rector or vicar; although that is not always the case.

The rector should be head of the altar guild, since ultimately the buck stops there, as far as the canonical responsibility for the ordering and conduct of all services. However, a rector will usually appoint a director or make some arrangements for leadership. Whomever the priest appoints should be a person with deep devotion to our Lord, someone who works well with others, knows what they are about in the sacristy, and with whom the rector works well.

While we are discussing the relationship between the priest and the altar guild, there is a key lesson that applies throughout the discussions of every module in this course. It is this: regardless of what this course states – or even what the rubrics in the Book of Common Prayer say – the duty of the altar guild is to serve, not correct the priest. Appointment to a parish altar guild is *not* the same as being consecrated as a bishop. It is the bishop's responsibility to correct a priest, if necessary.

GENERAL DUTIES

In general terms, the duty of the altar guild is to prepare all the things necessary for the celebration of the Eucharist or any of the other sacraments and offices of the church. All of these services can be found in the Book of Common Prayer (BCP) and the Book of Occasional Services. The preparations are done in a manner so that any service may be conducted in decency, order and beauty for the worship of Almighty God and his Son, Jesus Christ our Lord.

Members of the altar guild should always be mindful of the high privilege of serving God in his sanctuary. They must have a sincere devotion and a desire to make their work an acceptable offering to our Lord. In short, they must view their ministry as a sacred trust in conjunction with all the other members, not only of the altar guild, but of the entire parish.

The size of the parish or mission and the number of services offered determine the size of the altar guild and the organizational structure. As a general rule, altar guilds are divided into work teams that take turns doing their "holy house-work" on alternating Saturdays in preparation for the Sunday services. The members of each team then divide up the responsibility for any mid-week services that are scheduled during "their week."

MAKING USE OF TALENT

Historically, it was assumed that all guild members should be equally skilled in everything that needed to be done (i.e., flower arranging, polishing silver or brass, mending, sewing, ironing, dusting, vacuuming, etc.).

Though everyone knew it was not true, each person did his or her very best. Square pegs tried valiantly (sometimes tearfully) to squeeze into round holes, with varying degrees of success. The results were frequently years of quiet, devoted work done in utter frustration instead of joy. Prayers of thanksgiving offered for a calling to the ministry must often have been replaced by teeth-gritted prayers for strength to endure. This need not be the case!

No other job expects all workers to be equally competent in all phases of a project. Service on the altar guild need be no exception. Surely, duty rosters and schedules can be arranged to take advantage of God-given talents. For example, of the four altar guild teams at our parish, each had a DFA (designated flower arranger) – who had demonstrated either a talent or an interest in develop-ing the skill. Some parishes have an individual who takes responsibility for all flower arranging, regardless of the team on duty; others opt to have the flowers arranged by a local florist.

The best course of action is to access the talents and skills of the membership and adjust scheduling to balance the needs of the parish with the abilities of the altar guild.

The church cannot function at its best to the glory of God without a loyal, de-voted, loving altar guild. These loving servants, in their essential ministry, are truly servants of the servants of God.

SUMMARY

Altar Guilds are a relatively new ministry for laypeople, dating from the nineteenth century. Before that time minor orders of monks or laymen called *sacristans* performed the housekeeping chores in the churches. Sacristans were followed by parish clerks in the Church of England after the Reformation. In the middle of the 1800s, the parish clerk's duties were assumed by a group of volunteers who became known as the altar guild.

Early members of the altar guild were ladies of excellent repute. They looked upon their work as a sacred trust, but often made their work seem of such a pious nature that they frightened many away. We cannot allow myth, parish custom, legend, and other unwritten laws to create the illusion of a secret society.

Since men can do the same work in the sacristy and sanctuary, with as much interest, devotion, and dedication as women, guild membership should be open to both sexes.

The rector (or vicar) is the head of the altar guild. The liturgies of the church are his or her canonical responsibility. However, the priest usually appoints a person with deep devotion, who works well with others, to function in a leadership role.

The basic duties of the altar guild are to prepare the necessary things for celebration of the Eucharist and any of the other sacraments and offices of the church, so that they may be conducted in decency, order, and beauty.

Altar guild members should view their ministry as a sacred trust not only of the altar guild but of the entire parish.

Duty rosters and schedules should be arranged to take advantage of God-given talents. The church cannot function to the glory of God as smoothly without a loyal, devoted, loving altar guild.

If you feel comfortable with the information contained in this module, proceed to the Module 2 progress check; if not, you may want to review the module again before completing the progress check.

BE QUICK
TO
PRAISE
AND SLOW
TO
CRITICIZE.

MODULE 2
PROGRESS CHECK

Respond to the questions by filling in the blanks. No one is going to grade you, so feel free to use the text of the module to assist you in answering.

1. Nineteenth-century members of altar guilds were _____ of excellent repute who were not employed outside the home.

2. They looked upon their work as a _____ _____.

3. Altar guilds are a _____ for laypeople.

4. Minor orders of monks or laymen were called _____.

5. Altar guild membership should be open to _____ _____.

6. It is the rector's _____ _____ to be _____ of the altar guild.

(ANSWER SHEET ON BACK OF THIS PAGE)

MODULE 2
ANSWER SHEET

Respond to the questions by filling-in the blanks. No one is going to grade you, so feel free to use the text of the module to assist you in answering.

1. Nineteenth century members of altar guilds were **ladies** of excellent repute who were not employed outside the home.

2. They looked upon their work as a **sacred** trust.

3. Altar guilds are a **ministry** for laypeople.

4. Minor orders of monks or laymen were called **sacristans**.

5. Altar guild membership should be open to **both sexes**.

6. It is the rector's **canonical responsibility** to be **head** of the altar guild.

Now, look over your answers. If you feel comfortable that you understand the material in Module 2 continue to Module 3. If not, you may wish to review the material again.

MODULE 3
THE CHURCH BUILDING

*All backstage workers need to know the layout of the theater.
Sometimes the "show" requires costumes, lights, and props
placed in the audience before the show starts. The passion play
usually does, anyway.*

TIME:
Approximately one hour.

OBJECTIVE:
Given the contents of Module 3, you will be able to demonstrate an understanding of church buildings including their three principal points of focus by responding to simple fill-in-the blank questions within 10 minutes, with 100% accuracy.

ACTIVITIES:
- Read the text of the module
- Complete the Module Exercises
- Complete Progress Check

MATERIAL REQUIRED:
- This Module
- Pen or Pencil
- Progress Check

OTHER RESOURCE MATERIAL:
Your parish church

COURSE MAP

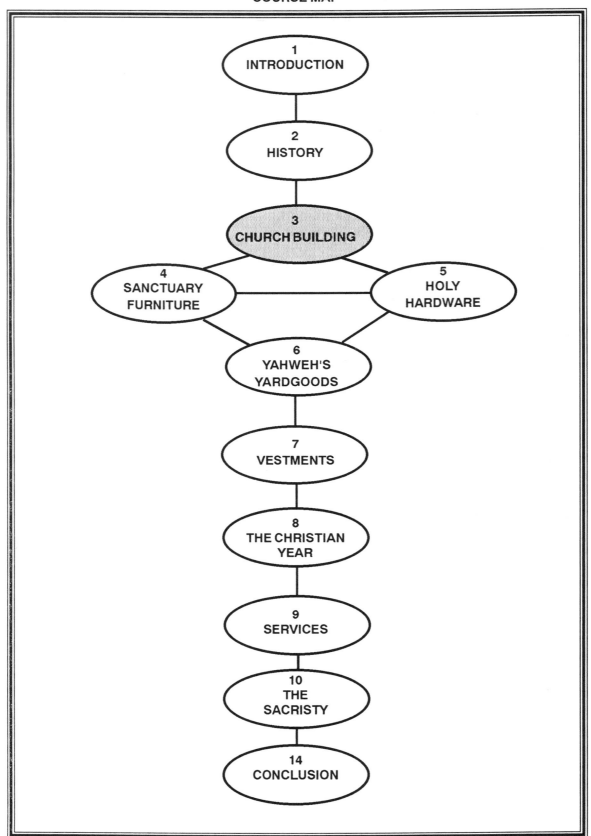

MODULE 3
THE CHURCH BUILDING

INTRODUCTION

Strictly speaking, the church building is constructed for the basic purpose of housing the altar, the center of our worship. Church buildings and church appointments (i.e., furniture, vessels, linens, etc.) should be attractive and *within* the financial means of the parish. Beauty and good taste need not be expensive!

Whatever the size or architecture of the Church building, all usually have the same basic identifiable parts. We Episcopalians, like all of catholic Christendom, are a people of symbols, even in architecture.

LITURGICAL SPACE

Most churches have are built with the altar at the east end of the building. The area of the church that is used for some act of public worship is sometimes referred to as "liturgical space." For the purposes of our lesson, the liturgical space is (moving from west to east) divided into:

- The Narthex
- The Nave
- The Choir
- The Sanctuary
- The Sacristy

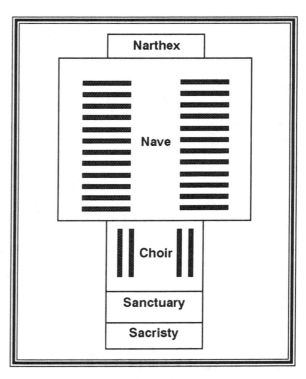

Fig. 3–1
Basic Liturgical Space

EXERCISE 3–1
IDENTIFYING LITURGICAL SPACE

Use this page to draw an outline of the liturgical space in *your* parish. Since each building is different, identify the narthex, nave, choir, sanctuary, and sacristy as it applies to your church building. Don't worry about the quality of your drawing (no one is going to see it, except you). For the best result, you should go into the church to complete this exercise. Sometimes drawing from memory results in forgotten, or out-of-proportion items.

SYMBOLISM OF THE ENTRYWAY

We enter the church and step into a narthex, a vestibule or entrance hall which may or may not be easily recognizable. The word narthex comes from the Greek *narthex*, meaning 'a large fennel,' (a tall herb). It symbolizes a place of waiting before baptism. Sometimes the baptismal font is located here. If not, then on leaving the narthex we will probably pass the

baptismal font. Every Christian is admitted to membership in the Body of Christ by baptism.

On your Exercise 3-1 Sheet, indicate the location of the font in your parish.

THE NAVE

Next is the nave (from the Latin word *navis,* meaning 'ship'), the largest part of the building and the central worship area, where we sit to be instructed from the lectern (in the front and to our right,

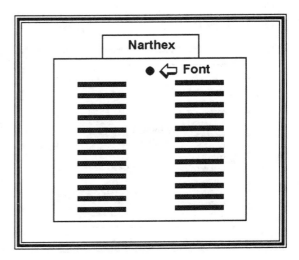

Fig. 3–2
Example of Font Location

as we face the altar) where the Old Testament, Psalm, and Epistle are read. You may hear this referred-to as the "epistle side." Also from the nave we receive instruction from the pulpit (in the front and to our left) from which the Gospel is preached; therefore, this is often referred to as the "gospel side."

Depending on the design of your church building, the seating in the nave may be permanent pews or folding chairs. All seating may face the same direction or be arranged in circular sections that may partially or completely surround the altar.

Your nave may have one large center aisle; a center and side aisles; or, where there are several sections, aisles separating each.

The aisles also play an important role in liturgical activity in the Nave. Entrance processions are frequently made from the Narthex, down the center aisle, to the sanctuary. The

Fig. 3–3
Basic Divisions of Nave

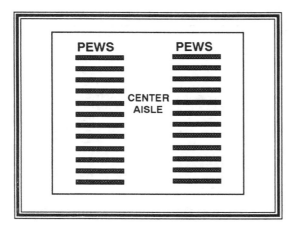

Fig. 3–4
Example of Basic Layout of Nave

Gospel reading is usually proclaimed from the midst of the people in the center aisle. The aisles are also used for the Great Litany, Stations of the Cross, and many other services, as well as for communicants to come to and depart from the altar rail during communion.

On your Exercise 3-1 Sheet, identify the seating (pews) and aisles in your church.

Shrines and Side Altars

In many cathedrals and even some larger parish churches (those that are built in the shape of a cross – a "cruciform"), the nave also may include additional side altars (along the side aisles), shrines (with or without candle racks), transepts (though not necessarily considered part of the nave), and even a lower altar and rail that may be located somewhere in the liturgical space: the narthex, nave, or sanctuary.

If your church has any (or all) of these, be sure to include them in your Exercise 3-1 line drawing.

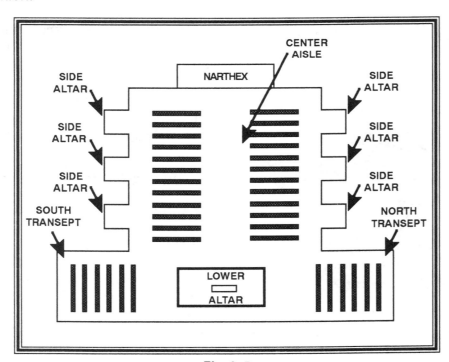

Fig. 3–5
Example of Cruciform Nave Features

THE CHANCEL

Chancel is from the Latin *cancelli* 'crossbars' and *cancellare* 'to enclose by a lattice.' The major features of the liturgical space that is called the chancel are: the pulpit, the lectern, the choir and the sanctuary. The chancel is that area immediately in front of and slightly raised above the nave. You most frequently see this layout in older structures and cathedrals.

The Lectern and the Pulpit

The Liturgy of the Word is presented from the lectern (from the Latin *lectrum,* for a 'reading desk') on the "epistle" side (i.e., the Old Testament reading, the Psalm, and the Epistle). The gospel side holds the pulpit (from the Latin *pulpitum,* meaning 'platform'), from which the Gospel is proclaimed. In other words, the sermon is preached here.

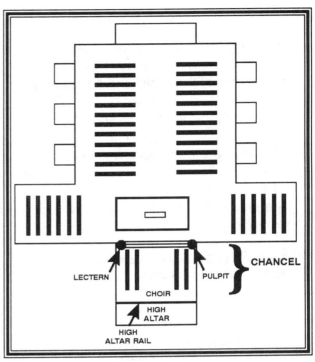

Fig. 3–6
Example of Cruciform Chancel

In some parishes there is only one lectern/pulpit and it may be located on either side. In these cases the lessons may be read from the pulpit, or perhaps from the middle of the nave (with the reader standing in place for the reading). Again, nothing is "set in concrete." (By the way, the seven most deadly words in the church are: **"WE NEVER DID IT THAT WAY BEFORE!"**)

The Choir

In some churches the choir sits in a section appropriately named the "choir," from the Greek word *khoros,* meaning 'a dance ring.' Especially in older churches and cathedrals that are built in a cruciform, the choir sits behind the chancel screen, between the nave and the altar. In churches built more recently the choir may be located at the back of the church, sometimes in

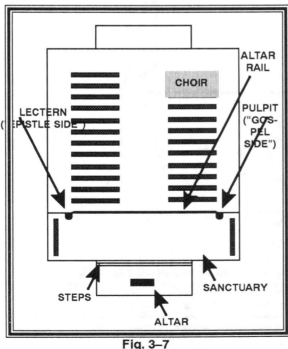

Fig. 3–7
Example of Less Complex Layout

a gallery. This is especially true in churches where the altar is placed in the center of the nave and completely (or partially) surrounded by the faithful — "church-in-the-round," so to speak.

Chances are that your parish church's chancel is much less complex than that of a cruciform church. However, the features of the chancel are present in some form.

So, on your Exercise 3-1 drawing indicate and identify the following:

- **The Pulpit**
- **The Lectern**
- **The Choir**
- **The Sanctuary**

The Sanctuary

The altar often stands at the east end of the church. The part of the church beyond the altar rail is called the sanctuary, from the Latin word *sanctus,* meaning 'holy.' The altar is usually raised above the rest of the church to emphasize its dignity as the Holy of Holies. The area on which it rests is sometimes called the "footpace" or "predella." *Predella* is an Italian word meaning 'footstool' or 'kneeling stool.'

We approach the altar after having been baptized, taught, and confirmed from the narthex, through the nave, to the sanctuary.

On your Exercise 3–1 drawing (if you have not already done so), identify the altar and the predella.

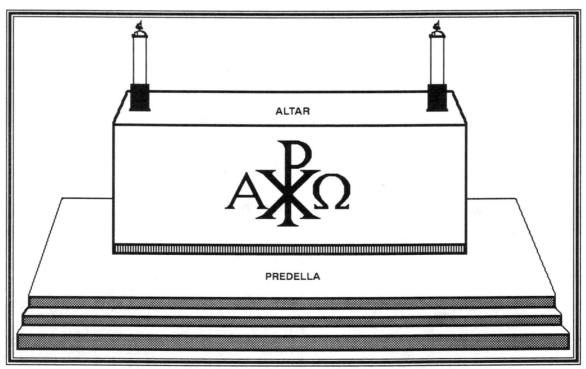

Fig. 3–8
The Altar and Predella

THE SACRISTY

Usually, somewhere adjoining or close to the sanctuary is located a room (or series of rooms) where the vestments, vessels, and other supplies necessary for the services are kept. The sacristy (from the Latin word *sacer,* meaning 'holy') is the non-observed liturgical space where the members of the altar guild do most of their preparatory and clean-up work. It is also the area where priests and servers gather and prepare for services. We will discuss the sacristy in greater detail as we continue the course.

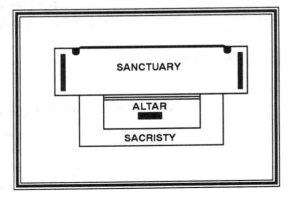

Fig. 3–9
Example of The Sacristy

Fig. 3–10
Examples of Church Architecture

For now, simply identify the sacristy (or sacristies) on your Exercise 3–1 drawing.

VARIATIONS IN BUILDINGS

Since the beginning of the liturgical movement in the early 1960s, some changes have come about in church architecture. For example, the baptismal font may now appear in the nave, closer to the chancel, rather than in the rear of the church. The choir may be situated wherever it is needed, depending upon the service. The nave may have flexible seating rather than fixed pews.

But whatever the changes, the three central focal points of worship (the font, the pulpit and the altar) will be in prominent places where everyone can easily see, hear, and participate in the actions taking place.

EXERCISE 3–2
INVESTIGATING YOUR PARISH'S LITURGICAL SPACE

Exercise 3–2 has two parts.

Part 1

First, using your Exercise 3–1 drawing, go back to the narthex. Beginning there notice the items that need to be cleaned, set up, refilled (i.e., holy water containers), etc. In other words, notice all of the things that require action by the altar guild. Write these responsibilities down either in the margin of your 3–1 drawing or on a separate sheet of paper.

From the narthex move to the nave, then to the sanctuary, and make the same type of notes for each. Save your lists to compare with actual check-off lists that your parish altar guild will provide.

Part 2

Using the Book of Common Prayer (or a copy of your parish service booklet) begin at the processional (from the narthex, if that's where processions begin) and walk through an entire worship service. Approach the altar. Stand where the clergy stand at various parts of the Eucharist. Stand at the font, as you read the baptismal service. Stand at the lectern and read aloud one of the lessons. You may gain an entirely new perspective. You will see what the celebrant, readers, and servers see – and perhaps understand more fully why some things must be placed in exactly the right position. It will give you a better "feel" for the acts of worship that you are helping to prepare.

SUMMARY

A church building is constructed for the purpose of housing the altar, the center of worship. Church buildings and church appointments should be attractive and within the financial means of the parish. The entryway, or Narthex, symbolizes a place of waiting before Baptism. Every Christian is admitted to membership in the Body of Christ through baptism.

The Nave is the central worship area of the church. The Lectern, to the right, where the Old Testament, Psalm, and Epistle are read, is sometimes called "the Epistle side." The pulpit, to the left, is often referred to as "the gospel side." In most parishes today the Gospel is usually read from the center aisle.

The part of the church beyond the altar rail is called the sanctuary. The riser upon which the altar sits is called the "footpace" or "predella." Some older churches have a section appropriately named the "choir" that is part of the "chancel." In churches built more recently the choir may be located at the back of the church, sometimes in a gallery.

Whatever the layout of your church building, the three principal points of worship – the font, the pulpit, and the altar – are located in prominent places.

If you feel comfortable with the information contained in Module 3, proceed to the Module 3 progress check; if not, you may want to review the module again before completing the progress check.

The Lord
is present
in his
Sanctuary,
Let us
praise
The Lord.

MODULE 3
PROGRESS CHECK

Respond to the questions by filling in the blanks. No one is going to grade you, so feel free to use the text of the module to assist you in answering.

1. The _____ is the largest part of the church building.

2. In churches built more recently _____ _____ may be located at the back of the church, sometimes in a gallery.

3. A church building is constructed for the purpose of_____ the
    _____.

4. The three major points of focus for worship in a church building are:

4a._____,

4b._____, and

4c._____.

(ANSWER SHEET ON BACK OF THIS PAGE)

MODULE 3
ANSWER SHEET

Respond to the questions by filling in the blanks. No one is going to grade you, so feel free to use the text of the module to assist you in answering.

1. The **nave** is the largest part of the church building.

2. In churches built more recently **the choir** may be located at the back of the church, sometimes in a gallery.

3. A church building is constructed for the purpose of **housing** the **altar**.

4. The three major points of focus for worship in a church building are:

4a.   the **font**,

4b.   the **pulpit**, and

4c.   the **altar**.

Now, look over your answers. If you feel comfortable that you understand the material in Module 3 continue to Module 4. If not, you may wish to review the material again.

MODULE 4
SANCTUARY FURNITURE

Your job as prop-person requires that you know what pieces of furniture are required for the play and where they are appropriately placed. Since the passion play has been running so long, some of these props have "funny" names. You need to understand what the names refer to.

TIME:
Approximately 30 minutes

OBJECTIVE:
Given the contents of Module 4, you will be able to demonstrate a knowledge of sanctuary furniture including (1) the altar, (2) names for different types of altar vestments, (3) types of altar crosses, and (4) other furniture used in the sanctuary, by responding to simple fill-in-the blank questions within 5 minutes with 100% accuracy.

ACTIVITIES:
- Read the text
- Complete Progress Check

MATERIAL REQUIRED:
- This Module
- Pen or Pencil
- Progress Check

OTHER RESOURCE MATERIAL:
None

COURSE MAP

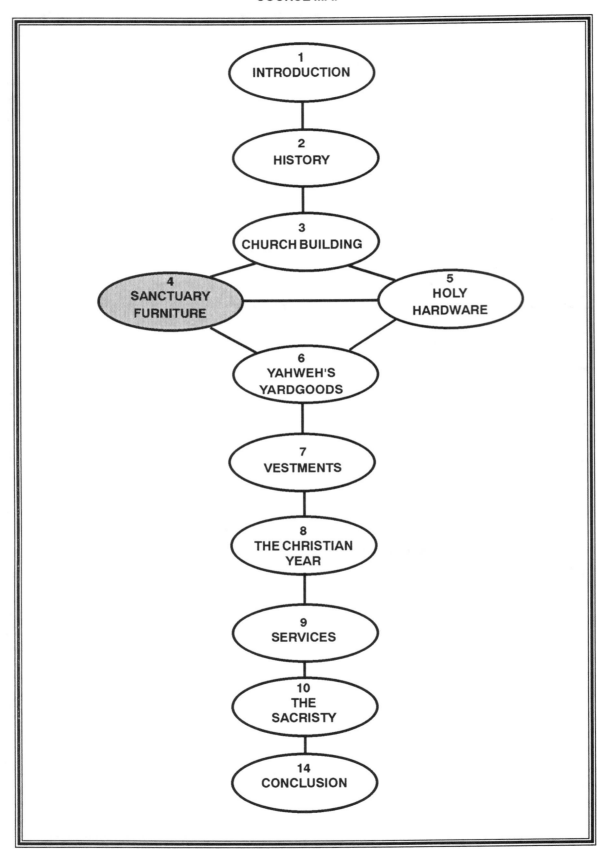

MODULE 4
SANCTUARY FURNITURE

INTRODUCTION

Regardless of the architecture of the church building, even in a storefront build-ing, there is an area called the sanctuary. It is the area, or liturgical space, in which the altar stands. The altar usually (but not always) stands behind an altar rail. It is usually (but not always) on a raised "platform," not only to emphasize its dignity and importance, but also to help the faithful see the action performed there and be more a part of it. In addition to the altar, the sanctuary may contain a tabernacle (or aumbry), various credence tables, a sanctuary lamp, a sedilia (seats for ministers and servers), and perhaps even a bishop's chair.

ALTAR

As we learned in the previous module, the altar rests on a *footpace* or *predella*, which is raised three steps above the sanctuary level. However, this also de-pends on the placement of the altar (such as in the round) and the architecture of the church. Regardless, the name of the platform remains the same.

The word *altar* comes from the low Latin word *altar, altare,* meaning (oddly enough) altar. Since the altar is the center of our worship, and our church build-ings are built to house it, all other parts of the building depend on the altar's placement. The altar should be freestanding (away from any wall) and com-pletely independent of the building itself. There should be adequate room for the celebrant to move completely around the altar and to celebrate facing the con-gregation.

Though there are still some parishes whose customs include the celebrant facing away from the congregation during the Eucharist, this practice is becoming more rare. If this is true of your parish, the positioning of credence tables and some of the vessels may vary accordingly.

There is no rule for the size of an altar. Each altar should be designed to propor-tions that suit the sanctuary in which it stands. However, it should be high enough, deep enough and long enough to fit its surroundings and allow enough room for the celebrant (or celebrants) to officiate. Normally, they are three feet four inches (forty inches) in height.

On a recent visit to an English cathedral, we noted a basement altar that was higher than this norm. The priest, who was small in stature, celebrated the Eucharist with his arms practically over his head just to reach the top of the altar. At the point in the mass where the elements are normally elevated, the poor man practically had to stand on tiptoe to get the chalice above the surface level of the altar.

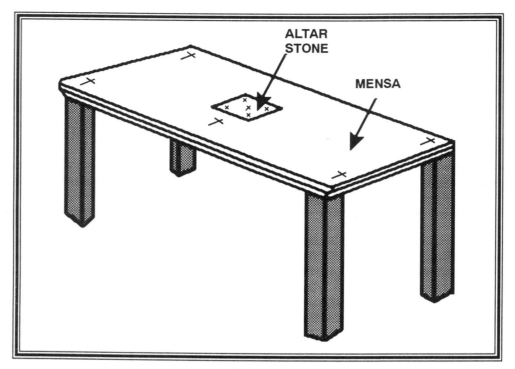

Fig. 4–1
Example of Basic Altar Mensa
With Altar Stone

The Mensa

The top of the altar is called the *mensa*. It is often marked or incised with five crosses, one in each corner and one in the center, symbolizing the five wounds in the body of our Lord. Some churches also have an altar stone, a separate stone set into the mensa containing a relic of a saint, although this is becoming extremely rare.

The altar is the center of the principal service of the church, the celebration of the Holy Eucharist, and should be made of the best material, either stone or wood, and of the finest workmanship the parish can afford, even if it is to be covered most of the time by a frontal, jacobean or laudian carpet. While we are discussing altar coverings, let's look at some of the ways we design "costumes" for the Table of the Lord.

Dressing the Altar

Good taste and fidelity to the surroundings should dictate the use of altar frontals. In some cases, altars beautifully carved and adorned with Christian symbols or scenes from the life of the Lord should *not* be covered. Or, if the simple beauty of the wood or stone enhances the setting, the altar should not be swathed in layers of damask.

Again, good taste should dictate if, when, or what kind of altar hangings are used. Sometimes a magnificent brocade frontal or superfrontal is totally out of keeping with the architecture and spirit of the parish, detracting from, rather than adding to its beauty.

Frontal

A frontal (from the Latin *frontalia*) is an altar covering that is a floor-length hanging, the length of the altar, usually the color of the day or the season. Or, if an altar is dedicated specifically, such as to the Blessed Virgin (in a Lady Chapel), or to the Holy Spirit, the frontal may be of the color identified with them (blue, in the case of the Blessed Virgin; red for the Holy Spirit, and so on). Since the material in a frontal is usually heavy, many times it is fastened by hooks to the underside of the mensa or supported in some other way.

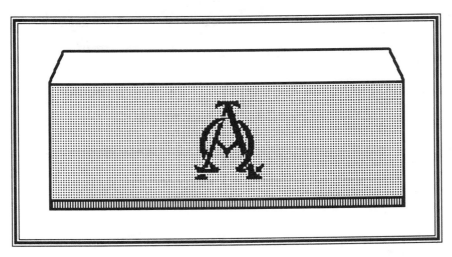

Fig. 4–2
Example of a Fitted, Laudian Frontal

Jacobean and Laudian Frontals

A *jacobean* frontal (anything *jacobean* refers to the time of James I of England) is usually heavy and completely covers a free standing altar and hangs to the floor like a huge tablecloth, with fullness at its corners.

A *laudian* frontal hangs like a jacobean, except it is fitted at the corners. The word *laudian* is most likely from the Latin word *laudare,* meaning 'praise.' This is as opposed to reference to Archbishop William Laud, who had his head lopped off by the Puritans. Occasionally, you may hear these frontals referred to as "carpets." This simply is a carryover from the time they were extremely heavy, and more carpet than brocade.

Superfrontal

A *frontlet* or *superfrontal* is a narrow strip of the same fabric and design as the frontal. It hangs from an undercloth of the altar, and covers (hides) the connections used to support the frontal. However, a superfrontal may be used alone to identify the seasonal color or color of the day, even if no frontal is used.

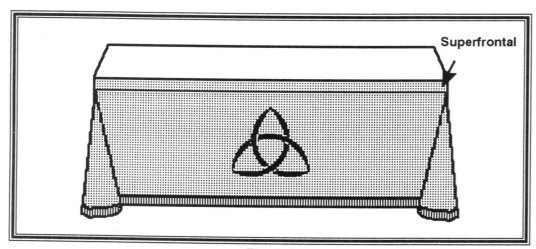

Fig. 4–3
Example of a Jacobean Frontal
with a Superfrontal

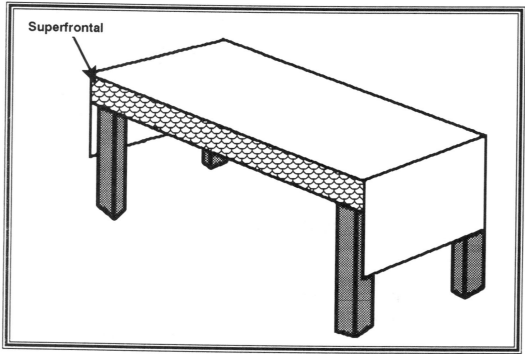

Fig. 4–4
Example of a Superfrontal
without a Frontal

In parishes where heavy, ornate frontals are used, the altar guild is usually delighted that they've been farsighted enough to include men in their membership because frontals are heavy and cumbersome to change.

REREDOS

Reredos is pronounced "rare-re-doss," from the Old French *arere,* meaning 'at the back,' and *dos* from the Latin *dorsum,* meaning 'back.' A reredos is a tall screen of wood or stone, usually carved with figures of the holy family, various Christian symbols, or saints that may stand behind the altar. Whatever else is on it, if anything, Christ, as the central figure of our faith and worship, should be the central prominent figure.

Fig. 4–5
Example of a Reredos

HANGINGS

Dossal: If you stand in front of an altar that is affixed to the wall and are confronted by a long heavy curtain, usually in old gold, deep burgundy or green, and that covers the area that would be taken by a reredos, it is called a *dossal* (pronounced *docile*).

Except in churches of ancient design and vintage, or those where the liturgical movement has made no inroads, are you likely to encounter:

Riddels: Tall curtains, usually matching the dossal, which enclose the altar at either end to furnish protection from drafts.

Canopies, Testers, or Baldacchinos: Hangings suspended from the ceiling or back wall and extending over the altar and footpace are called *canopies* or *testers*; or, if they are suspended from columns, they are called "baldacchinos" (pronounced "bald-a-kenos"). Bernini's baldacchino over the Papal Altar in St. Peter's, Rome, is probably the one most people know.

Fig. 4–6
Example of Altar with Plain Cross

ALTAR CROSSES

In the late Middle Ages, probably the sixteenth century, altar crosses assumed a prominent place in the sanctuary, being placed either on, behind, or above the altar.

When crosses were used, they were usually without decoration.

The oldest form of the crucifix is the *Christus Rex* (Christ the King), with royal robes and golden crown.

Fig. 4–7
Example of Christus Rex

The *Christus Patiens* (Suffering Christ) came into use later. All three types of altar crosses are used in the Episcopal Church. Care should be taken in the selection of the size of the cross or crucifix used, so that it does not over-power the altar and become the focus of attention.

Fig. 4–8
Example of Christus Patiens

RETABLE, GRADINE, OR SHELF

Some churches with freestanding altars close to the liturgical east wall may have a narrow shelf (called a *retable* or *gradine*) behind the altar against the wall. Originally, the gradine was a part of the reredos, which held the tabernacle, office lights, and, in some cases, flowers. Today they serve the same purpose, whatever form they take.

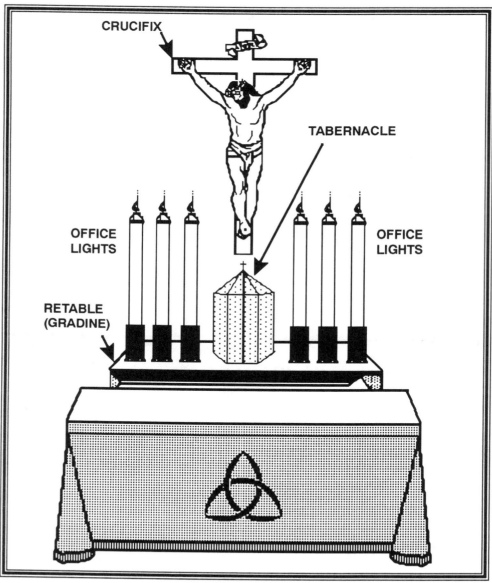

Fig. 4–9
Example of Altar and Gradine

TABERNACLE, AUMBRY, AND PYX

All three are basically safes, used as repositories or containers for the Reserved Sacrament (the consecrated bread and wine, the Body and Blood of our Lord) used by the clergy to communicate the sick and in time of emergency.

The *tabernacle* (from the Latin word *tabernaculum,* meaning 'tent') is a type of "Sacrament House" which sits on the retable (or gradine) behind the altar. It is lined with white linen and is often vested to match the altar hangings.

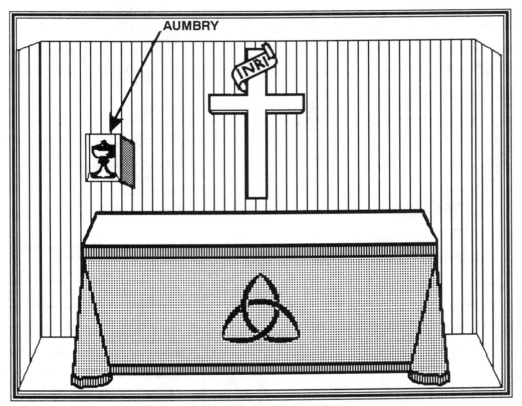

Fig. 4–10
Example of Aumbry

The *aumbry* (from the Latin *armarium,* meaning 'cupboard') is essentially a wall safe usually set into the wall on the gospel side of the sanctuary for the same purpose. A second aumbry may be provided in the sacristy to contain the *oleum Infirmorium* (oils for the sick) and chrism, used in baptism.

The *pyx* (from the Latin *pyxis*, meaning 'a box'), sometimes in the shape of a dove or flame, is hung near the altar and is used for reservation of the Blessed Sacrament. Today, however, most commonly the term "pyx" refers to a container (usually of silver or gold), about the size of a pocketwatch, that is used to take consecrated hosts to the sick or shut-in.

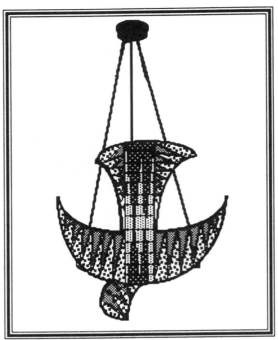

Fig. 4–11
Example of Stained-Glass Hanging Pyx With Shelf For Sacrament And Built-in Sanctuary Lamp

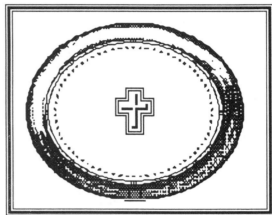

Fig. 4–12
Example of Pocket-sized Pyx

BISHOP'S CHAIR

The bishop's chair or throne is actually a misnomer since the bishop has only one throne, or *cathedra,* and that is located in his or her cathedral. It is usually a very dignified chair placed on the gospel side of the sanctuary when the bishop is present. In many parishes the "bishop's chair" is ordinarily used by the celebrant of the Eucharist.

SEDILIA

.The frequently backless bench on the epistle side of the chancel (or the sanctuary) for the officiating ministers and servers is called a *sedilia,* from the Latin plural *sedila,* meaning 'seat or stool.'

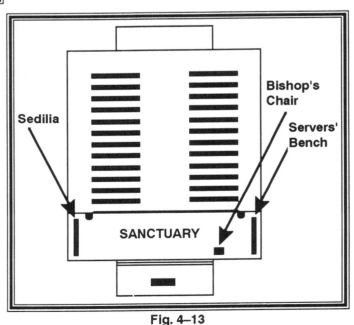

Fig. 4–13
Example of Locations of Sedilia and Bishop's Chair

CREDENCE TABLE

The credence table comes from medieval Latin *credentia,* meaning 'to believe, trust.' Originally a small side altar, it is a small table or shelf usually at the Epistle side of the altar. On it are placed the things used for the celebration of the Eucharist which are not, at first (if ever) placed directly on the altar. For example: a vested chalice; an extra chalice; the bread box; a lavabo bowl and towel; and extra cruets of wine.

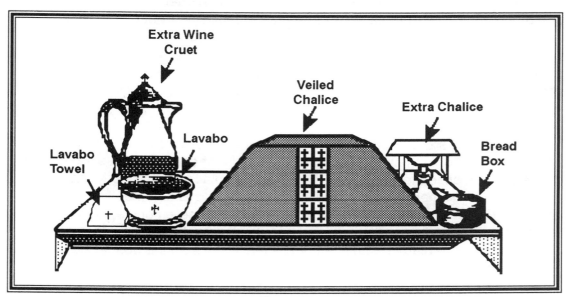

Fig. 4–14
Example of Credence Table
Or Credence Shelf Set-Up

Another credence table, covered with a white cloth, is often placed at the rear of the nave, on which the elements are placed for the offertory procession. The water and wine cruets usually flank the bread, but that is purely for aesthetics and for no other reason.

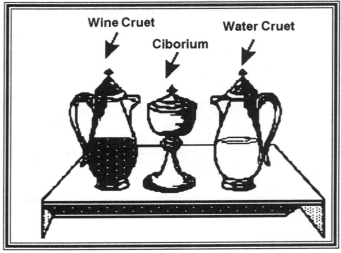

Fig. 4–15
Example of Credence Table
Set-Up In Nave

PRAYER DESK

The litany or prayer desk is a kneeling desk from which a litany is read, unless it is sung in procession. Most commonly it is placed in front of the sedilia for the celebrant's use. When used for a litany its place is on the floor of the nave at the chancel steps, if any, or thereabouts. Consult your rector or vicar.

PRIE-DIEU

A *prie-dieu* is a small piece of furniture that may be located in the sanctuary in one or all of the following places: in front of the sedilia; in front of server(s) benches; in front of members of the choir; and/or, in front of a bishop's chair. In the nave a prie-dieu may be located facing various shrines or side altars. The prie-dieu is basically a kneeler with an angled shelf (for holding books, etc.). The shelf also makes a dandy place to rest your elbows during deeply pious prayers.

THE MISSAL OR ALTAR BOOK

This rather good-sized book contains the service of the Eucharist in all its variations. It has not only the words but also the music for conducting a sung Eucharist. Thus, it is absolutely essential that it be in its place and properly marked for every service. Sometimes it is the lot of the altar guild to see that it is marked properly. Other times it will be the duty of a master of ceremonies, deacon or the celebrant. When not in use, the Missal and its stand, which is usually made of wood or metal, are placed on a shelf or credence table on the gospel side of the altar or in the sacristy.

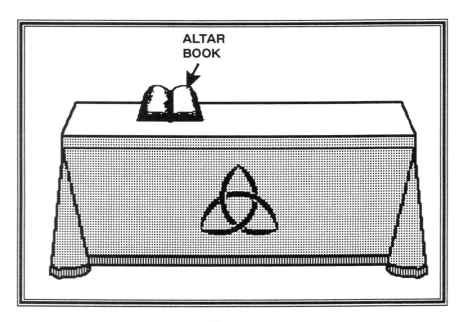

Fig. 4–16
Example of Altar with Altar Book

SUMMARY

In this module we have covered a lot of territory, but all material is centered on the furniture and "things" that you might find within the sanctuary at any Episcopal church.

For example, you have read that the *sanctuary* is simply the area in which the altar stands, that in many cases the altar rests on a *footpace* or *predella,* which is raised three steps above the sanctuary level; and that there should be adequate room for the celebrant to move completely around the altar.

The top of the altar is called the *mensa* and may be marked with five crosses, symbolizing the five wounds in the body of our Lord.

Good taste should dictate the use of altar frontals and hangings. A *frontal* is a floor length hanging, the length of the altar, usually of the color of the day or the season. A *superfrontal* is a narrow strip of the same fabric and design and covers the necessary hardware for hanging the frontal.

A *jacobean* frontal is heavy and completely covers a free standing altar hanging to the floor with fullness at its corners. A *laudian* frontal hangs like a jacobean, except it is fitted at the corners.

A *reredos* is a tall screen that may stand behind the altar. A long heavy curtain behind the altar is called a *dossal.* *Riddels* are tall curtains which enclose the altar at each end to furnish protection from drafts. *Canopies* and *testers* are hangings suspended from the ceiling or back wall and extending over the altar and footpace. If they are suspended from columns, they are called *baldacchinos.*

The oldest form of a crucifix is the *Christus Rex* (Christ the King), with royal robes and golden crown. The *Christus Patiens* or Suffering Christ came into use later.

A narrow shelf behind the altar is called a *retable* or *gradine*.

A *tabernacle* , an *aumbry* and a *pyx* are used as repositories for the Reserved Sacrament. A tabernacle sits on the gradine (or retable) behind the altar, is lined with white linen, and is often vested to match the altar hangings. An aumbry is set into the wall on the gospel side of the sanctuary. A pyx is sometimes in the shape of a dove or flame, and is hung suspended near the altar.

Also in Module 4, you have covered other sanctuary furniture including:
- The *bishops chair* which is usually placed on the gospel side of the sanctuary when the bishop is present.

- A *sedilia*, or a backless bench is located on the epistle side of the sanctuary for the officiating ministers and servers.

- *Credence tables* are small tables or shelves (usually on the epistle side of the altar) that are used for things used in the celebration of the Eucharist. Frequently, a credence table is placed at the rear of the nave for the elements carried in the offertory procession.

- The *litany desk* or *prayer desk* is a kneeling desk from which a litany is read, unless it is sung in procession. Most commonly it is placed in front of the sedilia for the celebrant's use.

- A *prie-dieu* is an individual kneeler with an angled shelf for holding books, etc.

- The *Altar Book* contains not only the words but also the music used in a sung Eucharist. It should be in its place and properly marked for every service.

Now, if you feel comfortable with the information contained in this module, proceed to the Module 4 progress check; if not, you may want to review the module again before completing the progress check.

MODULE 4
PROGRESS CHECK

Respond to the questions by filling in the blanks. No one is going to grade you, so feel free to use the text of the module to assist you in answering.

1.   The _____ is simply the area in which the altar stands.

2.   A _____ _____ is heavy and completely covers a freestanding altar, hanging to the floor with fullness at its corners.

3.   The top of the altar is called the _____.

4.   The _____ _____ contains not only the words but also the music used in a sung Eucharist.

5.   The oldest form of a crucifix is the _____ _____.

(ANSWERS ON THE BACK OF THIS PAGE)

MODULE 4
ANSWER SHEET

1.   The **sanctuary** is simply the area in which the altar stands.

2.   A **jacobean frontal** is heavy and completely covers a freestanding altar, hanging to the floor with fullness at its corners.

3.   The top of the altar is called the **mensa**.

4.   The **altar book** contains not only the words but also the music used in a sung Eucharist.

5.   The oldest form of a crucifix is the **Christus Rex**.

Now, look over your answers. If you feel comfortable that you understand the material in Module 4 continue to Module 5. If not, you may wish to review the material again.

MODULE 5
HOLY HARDWARE

All plays have small props that the backstage crew are respon-sible for, too. On stage, if a telephone rings and the actor reaches to answer it (only to discover that the prop people have neglected to set the telephone in place), the audience can imagine a telephone. It is very difficult for a congregation to imagine a chalice.

TIME:
Approximately 45 minutes

OBJECTIVE:
Given the contents of Module 5, you will be able to demonstrate an understand-ing of the appointments in the sanctuary of a church including (1) vessels used in the celebration of the Eucharist, and (2) proper use of lights and candles, by responding to simple fill-in-the-blank questions with 100% accuracy.

ACTIVITIES:
- Read the text in the module
- Complete Progress Check

MATERIAL REQUIRED:
- This Module
- Pen or Pencil
- Progress Check

OTHER RESOURCE MATERIAL:
None

COURSE MAP

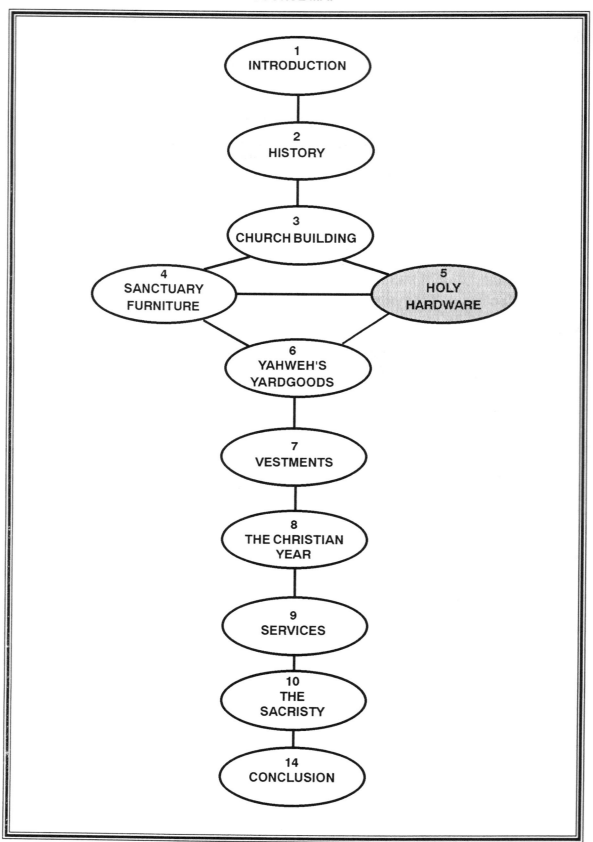

MODULE 5
HOLY HARDWARE
(or, The Vessels Used in the Church)

INTRODUCTION
The venerable vessels that are used in services of the church differ in style and materials from parish to parish. Some are made of silver and gold; some are even bejeweled. On the other hand, some parishes have vessels made of pottery. The simplicity or elegance of the "holy hardware" is usually consistent with that of the parish architecture and style. Whatever the style of these utensils, their function is basically the same.

THE CHALICE
From the Latin *calix* and the Greek *kalyx,* both meaning 'cup,' this vessel is a cup which is used at the altar to hold the elements of wine and water for consecration and communion. Most commonly, the chalice has been a large, tall, beautiful vessel of silver, lined with a mask of gold. However, some parishes now use chalices of ceramic or crystal. The Mass (Eucharist) is valid regardless of the materials used for the chalice.

Fig. 5–1
Example of a Chalice

The chalice is oftentimes the most prized possession of a parish and may be embossed, engraved, enameled, or even jeweled. Most parishes have more than one chalice, and some use more than one chalice during a Eucharist. It is customary, as stated in the Book of Common Prayer and preferred by liturgical experts, that only one chalice be on the altar until after the breaking of the bread. However, do as your clergy directs (even if the BCP says otherwise!).

Fig. 5–2
Example of a Paten

THE PATEN

The *paten*, from the Latin *patena,* meaning 'pan or shallow dish,' is a plate made of silver, gold, or ceramic to match the chalice and upon it is placed the priest's wafer when the chalice is vested for Eucharist. (Remember: the term "wafer" is used when referring to eucharistic bread before it is consecrated. After it is consecrated, it is the "Host.")

Some patens have a deep center that fit the lip of their matching chalice. However, some are relatively flat. A priest usually has a personal preference of the style of paten that is used. So, if your altar guild elects to purchase a new set of vessels, you should talk with the clergy before buying something that the clergy will not use.

THE CIBORIUM

The *ciborium* is a Latin word meaning 'drinking cup.' It resembles the chalice (in fact may be identical) except that it has a lid. It is used to hold the bread (wafers) at the Eucharist. It is brought to the altar at the offertory, and may be used in reservation of the Sacrament in the aumbry or tabernacle. Most churches that no longer use wafers (preferring real bread instead) have also stopped using the ciborium.

Fig. 5–3
Example of a Ciborium

CRUETS, FLAGONS, AND EWERS

Cruets are usually of glass (or crystal) so that the deacon or server can easily tell which is water and which is wine. If, however, your parish uses matching silver, pewter, or ceramic cruets, the identity crisis can be solved quite handily by putting a tiny red dot of paint or tape on the one containing wine.

Fig. 5–4
Example of Cruets

Fig. 5–5
Example of Flagons

Flagons are usually larger than cruets and eliminate the need for extra cruets at a large service. They are frequently made of silver or pewter. Therefore, the water and wine cannot always be seen in a flagon. A simple technique for distinguishing which flagon is which, is to place a small colored dot on the base of the flagon that holds the wine.

Fig. 5–6
Example of a Ewer

Ewers are vase-shaped pitchers that are commonly made of pewter or silver. They also can be used to hold the water and wine for the Eucharist. Frequently, a ewer is used to hold the water for a baptism prior to its being blessed and poured into the font.

Selection of cruets, flagons, and ewers should be based not only on style but, more important, on ease of handling.

BREAD BOX

A *bread box* is a small, chambered box, usually silver, which is set near the altar (i.e., on the credence table) and contains extra wafers. Each priest and altar guild decides how many wafers will be in it, and how they will be grouped to avoid tedious counting at the altar.

Fig. 5–7
Example of a Bread Box

CARE OF HOLY HARDWARE

A word about the care of these vessels seems in order here. After a Eucharist, rinse the chalice(s) with boiling water and pour the contents (and excess water) down the piscina. Wash all the vessels with mild soap and warm water and dry them with a soft cloth. These actions should keep the metal vessels in fine shape. Polish silver items as needed, of course, but too much polishing of silver can mar the surface and require frequent and costly replating. If you use silver cruets, rinse them after each service, then put a soft tissue or paper towel in them to absorb excess moisture.

The care and feeding of brass is another matter altogether. All brass items, unless lacquered, need regular polishing – in other words, every time they are used. Brasso is a reputable old brass polish, but there are others. Just be very sure that every last bit of polish is completely removed each time, or the brass will not shine well and will hold fingerprints. Say your prayers if you ever use brass polish on a lacquered brass surface!

OTHER APPOINTMENTS IN THE SANCTUARY

In addition to eucharistic vessels, other appointments that do not specifically fall into the category of "holy hardware" include (1) Alms Basins; (2) the Sanctus Bell; (3) the Thurible; (4) an Incense Boat; (5) Processional Cross and Torches; and (6) the Monstrance.

ALMS BASINS

The collection plates (to be crass), or *alms basins* (from Old English *aelmysse* through Latin, meaning 'mercy and pity') are usually made of brass or silverplate, and differ in size and style according to the desires and means of the parish. Many feature velvet (or needlepoint) pads in the bottom, presumably to prevent the clatter of small change from disturbing the musical interlude that usually accompanies the collection of alms.

We are aware of at least one parish that owns several large, beautiful, custom-designed, silverplated alms basins that were donated as a memorial. They are still kept in the hand-made velvet bags designed for them and they are hidden away in a drawer in the sacristy. The altar guild does not believe them to be representative of the "simple style" of the (rather large) parish. Most of the parishoners are unaware that they exist.

Since brass and silver alms basins must be polished regularly, perhaps the real reason they are not used has less to do with the "simple style" of the parish and more to do with the required altar guild "elbow-grease." At any rate, they were given to the glory of God in someone's memory. Unless they are used, they neither glorify our Lord nor is the person remembered. Perhaps they should be passed on to a parish that needs them and would gratefully use them.

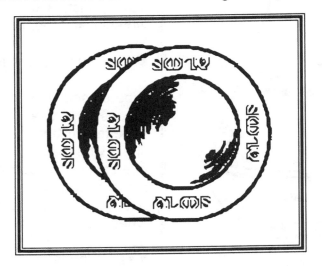

Fig. 5–8
Example of Alms Basins

SANCTUS BELLS AND GONGS

Many modern parishes have never seen *sanctus bells*, much less a *sanctus gong*. They may be made of brass or even silver, and are used at the Sanctus *(Holy, Holy, Holy Lord)* in the Mass; at the elevation of the elements; and to summon the people to make their communion.

Sanctus bells (actually from one to four bells) have a handle and are twisted quickly to cause the ring. A sanctus gong is larger and is struck with some type of mallet.

Tradition says that their use began when the Mass was in Latin, rather than native languages. The bells were a means by which the people were able to identify the "holy" times of the Eucharist and act accordingly.

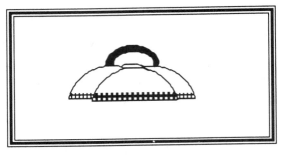

Fig. 5–9
Example of Sanctus Bell

Fig. 5–10
Example of Sanctus Gong

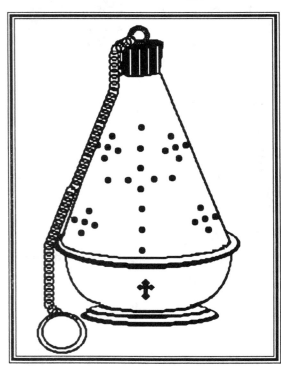

Fig. 5–11
Example of Thurible

THURIBLE

The *thurible,* (also called a *censer*) is the vessel in which incense is burned on charcoal. Thuribles are used by some parishes as a regular part of their worship. In other parishes, they are used only on special occasions. And in some churches they are never used.

Where used, they may be carried in processions, used to cense the altar, used to cense the Gospel Book at the time of the reading of the Gospel, and even during the consecration. The rector of your parish will pretty well determine when and where – and on what occasions – the thurible will be used. The thurible is not to be confused with the person in charge of it. He or she is called a *thurifer*.

INCENSE BOAT

The thurible is accompanied by a separate container for the incense called an *incense boat,* which contains a spoon for spooning small lumps of incense into the thurible.

Fig. 5–12
Example of Incense Boat

ABOUT USING BELLS AND INCENSE

Without going into great detail about the "rights" and "wrongs" of the use of "bells and smells" in liturgical services of the church, as a general rule, both are used in churches that are considered "high" Episcopal churches – or churches with a more Anglo-Catholic tradition.

The only altar guild consideration for the bells is that they (the bells, not the altar guild) usually require polishing. Whether brass or silver, they can be professionally "sealed" to reduce the maintenance time and save the finish (again, on the bells, not the altar guild – regardless of what you think!).

A couple of considerations should be given to the safe use of a thurible. First, the preparation area (where the charcoal is stored and the fire started) should be surrounded by fireproof materials. Most charcoal used for thuribles is "self-starting." Therefore, even a small spark can cause an entire box of charcoal to ignite. Even if it's not the specific responsibility of the altar guild to prepare the thurible, it is a good practice to double-check the preparation area to assure safety.

Another consideration is to keep a metal dustpan and flame-retardant broom (of some type) in a location close to the sacristy. It is not uncommon for the thurifer to drop the thurible or for the fire to fall out of the thurible during a service. Having something handy to clean up the fire not only is a safety factor, but also allows minimal disruption of the service.

PROCESSIONAL CROSS

The *processional cross* is a cross of some beauty and importance affixed to a staff and carried high. It is usually, but not always, preceded or flanked by torch-bearers as it leads the procession into the church. It may also lead gospel and offertory processions, and retiring processions at the end of the Eucharist or Mass. (Please note the term "retiring processions." Unless the altar party *backs* out of the church, it is *not* a *recessional.*)

Processional crosses may be (and usually are) used at weddings, funerals, and other occasional services.

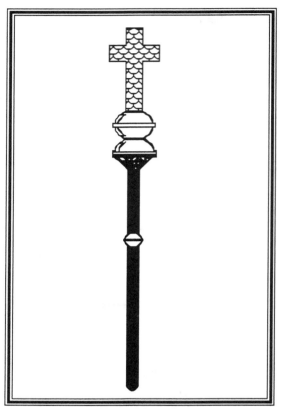

Fig. 5–13
Example of a Processional Cross

Fig. 5–14
Example of Torches

TORCHES

Frequently made of brass, torches are simply candle holders that are affixed to a staff. Depending on the parish, there may be two, four, or six torches for a service. They come in pairs, based on the availability of torch-bearers and the supply of torches possessed by the church.

ABOUT PROCESSIONAL CROSSES AND TORCHES

Depending on the material (brass, wood, silver,etc.) and the design of the processional cross, it will most likely need some amount of cleaning and maintenance. If made of silver or brass, it also can be professionally "sealed" to preserve the finish and save wear and tear on the altar guild.

The server that carries the processional cross is called a *crucifer*. Though usually not in the realm of altar guild responsibilities, the crucifer should be cautioned about moving in and out of doors with the processional cross. Banging it into doorframes can damage the cross as well as the doorframe! Besides, we never want to read a headline that says, "Altar Guild Member Impaled in Sacristy!" Also, if your church has ceiling fans, carrying the processional cross too high can be hazardous!

No one knows the number of altar guild members who have had to do penance for their thoughts about young torchbearers who "play" with the followers on wax candle torches, thereby dripping hot wax all over the torch. Especially with brass torches, wax drippings are a constant problem. Wishing ill toward the torchbearers does not help – but inviting the parents to join the altar guild frequently resolves the problem!

MONSTRANCE

Another item that falls generally under the category of a vessel is the *monstrance,* which some churches still use. Its ritual use began around the late thirteenth century. The word monstrance comes from the Latin *monstrare,*

meaning 'to show.' Usually of gold and/or silver, in a cruciform shape with a clear glass (or crystal) circular receptacle at its center (from which sunlight appears to radiate), the monstrance is designed to hold a consecrated Host that is exposed for adoration. The monstrance is used to contain the Host as it is carried during the liturgy of Solemn Benediction.

Fig. 5–15
Example of a Monstrance

LIGHTS (as in 'Let There Be') OR CANDLES

Candles have been used in Christian worship from the beginning, but no symbolic meaning was attached to them until the Middle Ages. Since then there has been so much variation in numbers and placement of lights that one could use almost any number with relative impunity. Thankfully, the American church, of late, has a leaning toward the tendency that "fewer are more effective."

SANCTUARY LAMP

The most obvious candle, the *sanctuary lamp,* hangs near the aumbry or tabernacle and is kept ever-burning to mark the presence of the Reserved Sacrament. It is only put out when the Sacrament is removed. If it should accidently go out, don't panic. Just relight it.

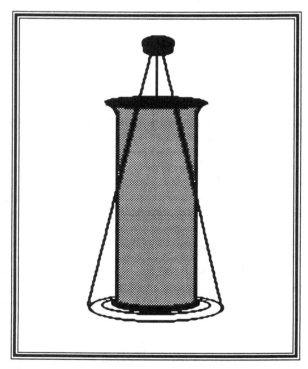

Fig. 5–16
Example of a Sanctuary Lamp

EUCHARISTIC LIGHTS

Two large *eucharistic lights* are placed on the altar during celebration of the Eucharist. Proper use of eucharistic lights includes their use for all Eucharists, regardless of other candles or lights used. However, again, your rector is your guide. The candles and candlesticks used as eucharistic lights should be large enough to be seen, but not so large or tall as to draw undue attention to themselves. They should enhance, not overpower, the altar.

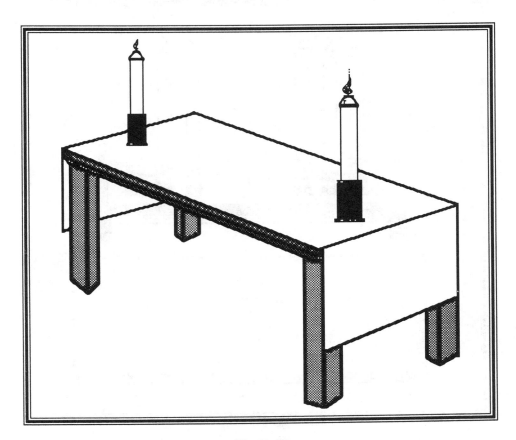

Fig. 5–17
Example of Eucharistic Lights on Altar

OFFICE LIGHTS

The *office lights* are candles of medium height which may be placed either on a gradine or retable (usually three to a side) or beside the altar. The term "office lights" is a misnomer. The office lights are really there (whether lighted or not) to indicate that the Sacrament is reserved. Although they do not have to be lighted for the Eucharist, they may be.

Fig. 5–18
Example of Office Lights on Gradine

CANDELABRA

Candelabra are lights (usually seven branches) used for special occasions such as Christmas, Pentecost, Easter, and weddings and are generally placed behind the altar on the gradine or near the altar.

Fig. 5–19
Example of Candelabra

BISHOP'S CANDLE

A *bishop's candle* is a single candle which may be placed on the altar in addition to the eucharistic lights when the bishop celebrates the Eucharist.

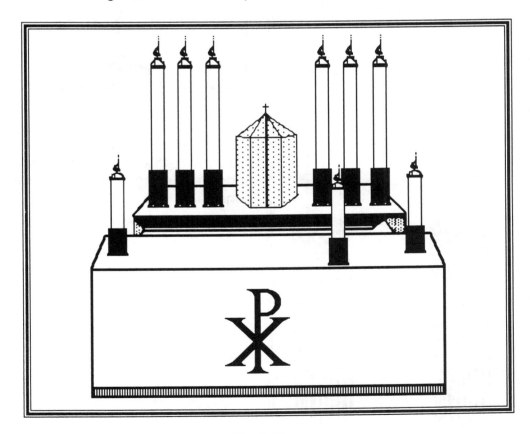

Fig. 5–20
Example of Altar Light
Set-Up with Bishop's Candle

PASCHAL CANDLE

The *paschal candle* is lighted at the Easter Vigil and stands in the sanctuary until Pentecost. Then it may stand by the font to be used at baptisms, or placed in the sanctuary during a Requiem Mass.

Fig. 5–21 (right)
Example of Paschal Candle

Fig. 5–22 (below)
Example of Pavement Lights

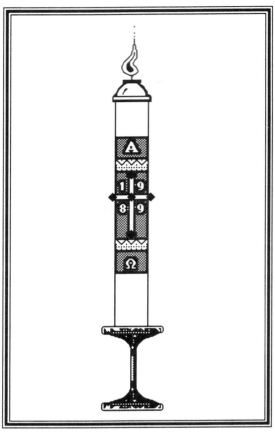

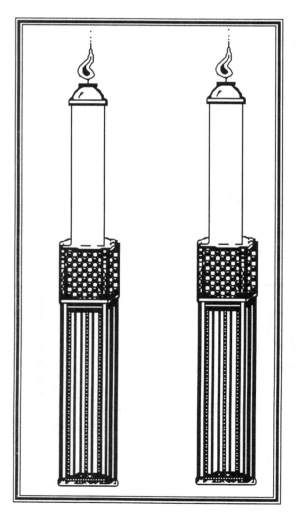

PAVEMENT LIGHTS

pavement lights are any large pair of candles standing on the floor of the sanctuary.

BIER LIGHTS

Bier lights are tall candlesticks which stand on the nave floor beside a coffin during the Burial Office. There may be two, four, or six of them, used in pairs. Frequently the paschal candle is also used during funerals.

Fig. 5–23
Example of Use of Bier Lights
with Paschal Candle

Now that we have shed quite enough light on the subject of candles, dear souls, we shall move on to a summary of what we have covered in this module.

SUMMARY

In this module we have covered appointments in addition to furnishings, including alms basins, the sanctus bell, the thurible, the processional cross (or crosses), and torches.

We have also defined the vessels used in the church, including:

- The Chalice – a cup which is used at the altar to hold the wine and water for consecration and communion.

- The Paten – a plate made of silver, gold, or ceramic to match the chalice. Upon it is placed the priest's wafer when the chalice is vested for Eucharist.

- The Ciborium – a cup which looks like the chalice, except it has a lid and is used to contain the bread at the Eucharist.

- Cruets – containers for the water and wine, usually made of glass or crystal.

- Flagons – containers that are most often larger than cruets and eliminate the need for extra cruets at a large service.

- Ewers – pitchers which can be used in place of cruets or flagons, and to hold water at baptisms.

- A Bread Box – a small box, usually silver, containing extra wafers.

We also discussed the use of candles and lights in the sanctuary, noting that:

- The sanctuary lamp, hangs near the aumbry or tabernacle and is kept ever-burning to mark the presence of the Reserved Sacrament.

- Eucharistic lights are placed on the altar during a celebrations of the Eucharist.

- Office lights are placed either on a gradine or retable (usually three to a side), or beside the altar.

- Candelabra are lights (usually with seven branches) used for special occasions such as Christmas, Pentecost, Easter, and weddings and are generally placed behind the altar on the retable or near the altar.

- A bishop's candle is a single candle placed on the altar in addition to the eucharistic lights, when the bishop celebrates the Eucharist.

- Bier lights are all candlesticks which stand on the nave floor beside a coffin.

- The paschal candle is lighted at the Easter Vigil and stands in the sanctuary until Pentecost.

- Pavement lights are any large pair of candles standing on the floor of the Sanctuary.

Now, if you feel comfortable with the information contained in Module 5, proceed to the progress check. If not, you may wish to review the module again before completing the progress check.

OUR LIVES
ARE THE
VESSELS
OF THE
HOLY SPIRIT

MODULE 5
PROGRESS CHECK

Respond to the questions by filling in the blanks. Feel free to use the text of the module to assist you in answering.

1. The_____ _____ is affixed to a staff and leads the procession into the church.

2. The_____ is a cup which is used at the altar to hold the wine and water for _____ and communion.

3. The_____ _____ hangs near the aumbry or tabernacle and is kept ever-burning to mark the presence of the _____.

4. Eucharistic lights should be used on the altar during all _____.

(ANSWERS ON THE BACK OF THIS SHEET)

MODULE 5
ANSWER SHEET

Respond to the questions by filling in the blanks. Feel free to use the text of the module to assist you in answering.

1. The **processional cross** is affixed to a staff and leads the procession into the church.

2. The **chalice** is a cup which is used at the altar to hold the wine and water for **consecration** and communion.

3. The **sanctuary lamp** hangs near the aumbry or tabernacle and is kept ever-burning to mark the presence of the **Reserved Sacrament**.

4. Eucharistic lights should be used on the altar during all **Eucharists**.

Now, look over your answers. If you feel comfortable that you understand the material in Module 5, please continue to Module 6. If not, you may wish to review the material again.

MODULE 6
YAHWEH'S YARDGOODS

The overall set design is much more than just furniture and small props. Little touches like tablecloths, scarves, etc. make the set look as if real people live there. You certainly wouldn't invite important people into your home for dinner and refuse them a napkin. So, to make the stage "real" for the presence of the Most Important Guest and those who participate, let's completely "dress" the stage.

TIME:
Approximately 30 minutes

OBJECTIVE:
Given the contents of Module 6, you will be able to demonstrate an understanding of the types of linens used in the Eucharist by responding to simple fill-in-the-blank questions with 100% accuracy.

ACTIVITIES:
- Read the text of the module
- Complete Progress Check

MATERIAL REQUIRED:
- This Module
- Pen or Pencil
- Progress Check

OTHER RESOURCE MATERIAL:
None

COURSE MAP

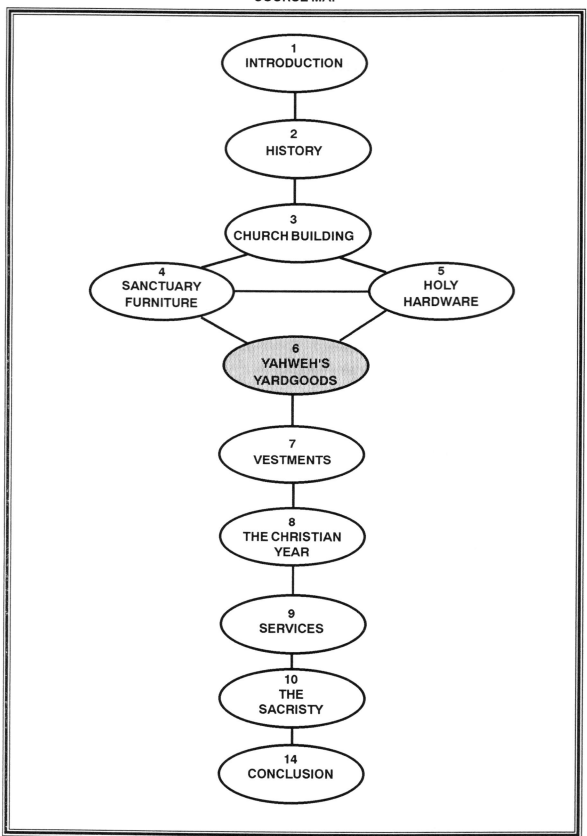

MODULE 6
YAHWEH'S YARDGOODS

INTRODUCTION

The word "linen" is now used as a convenient general term to describe the various cloths used, rather than as an actual description of a type of material, since real linen is no longer universally used for *fair linens, corporals, purificators,* and *lavabo* or *baptismal towels.*

The custom of covering the table or altar with a cloth for the Eucharist can be documented as early as the second century. And, as is true in almost all the areas we have discussed thus far, custom and need have had a real impact on the evolution of altar linens as well.

CERECLOTH

The top of the altar may be covered with a *cerecloth* – a waxed linen the exact size of the altar slab. Since waxed linen is so difficult to prepare and not easily found these days, for practical purposes a plastic or flannel waterproof sheeting is used. Its purpose is to protect the fair linen from the dampness that is characteristic of stone altars, or stains from wooden ones. However, the use of a cerecloth is optional. Today, there are ways of sealing stone and wood so that they do not bleed or stain.

SECOND LINEN

Lying on top of the cerecloth, if used, is another linen called a *second linen* made the exact length and width of the altar to which superfrontals are sometimes attached.

FAIR LINEN

The linen on top of the altar is called the *fair linen.* It covers the entire top of the altar and may hang down over the ends to any length, even to the footpace. Sometimes it is embroidered in white with five crosses, or other fitting Eucharistic symbols, at the four corners and in the center. It is covered, when the altar is at rest (not being used), by a dust cover of some suitable fabric which should be large enough to shield the fair linen completely. It may be of the same color. (Just remember to remove it when vesting the altar for a service! We can tell you about a glorious Easter Vigil and Mass celebrated atop the dust cover!)

CORPORAL

Eventually the *corporal* developed. It is a ninefold "placemat" to protect the fair linen and to catch any consecrated particles or drops of wine which might fall on it during the Eucharist. This large square of "linen" takes its name from the Latin *corpus* (meaning body). It is unfolded and placed on the altar under the chalice.

PALL

A second corporal placed over the chalice (originally to keep insects out) was eventually stiffened and today is called a *pall*. (One might wonder if that was the origin of the word *appalled*. Though it's not, I would certainly be appalled to find an insect floating around in the chalice!)

PURIFICATOR

The *purificator* was developed to purify – cleanse or wipe – the lip of the chalice after each person is communicated. Considerably smaller than a corporal, a purificator is also used to clean the chalice and paten during the ablutions (cleaning done at the altar by the sacred ministers as part of the service, after communion).

A pattern has emerged hasn't it? For any service we need something to set the chalice and paten on, something to cover them, and something to use to clean up: corporal, pall and purificator.

LAVABO TOWEL

The *lavabo towel* is folded and placed across the lavabo bowl to be used when the celebrant washes his or her fingers during the offertory.

VEIL AND BURSE

Not considered altar linens, but rather part of the eucharistic vestments, the *veil* and the *burse* are covered here because of their usage.

The *veil* matches the vestments worn by the celebrant and is a covering for the communion vessels. In some parishes where the chalice is not placed on the altar until the offertory, the use of a veil is being abandoned.

The use of a *burse* is utilitarian. The name itself becomes easy to remember if we just think of the word purse. It is a case placed on top of the veiled communion vessels to hold the corporal and extra purificators. It matches the chalice veil.

VESTING THE CHALICE

No doubt there is a diagram on the wall of your sacristy showing the order in which things are done to prepare the holy hardware for celebration of the Eucharist. Study it. It's really very easy.

Let's go through preparing the chalice in step-by-step fashion.

STEP 1   Get the chalice and drape a purificator across the top of it.

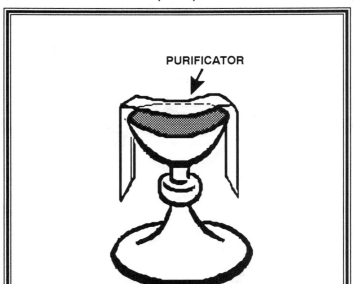

Fig. 6–1
Example of Chalice and Purificator

STEP 2   Place the paten on top of the purificator.

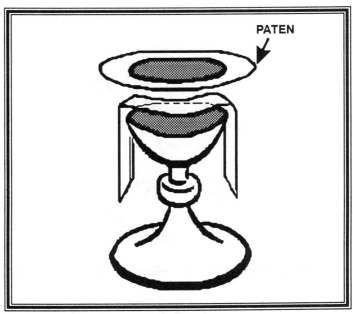

Fig. 6–2
Example of Chalice, Purificator and Paten

STEP 3   Place the priest's wafer on the paten. The priest's wafer is larger (approximately three inches in diameter) than the wafers used for the congregation.

Fig. 6–3
Example of Chalice, Purificator, Paten
and Priest's Wafer

STEP 4   Cover it with a pall.

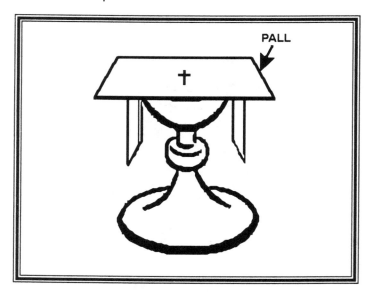

Fig. 6–4
Example of Placement of Pall

STEP 5 Drape it with the veil.

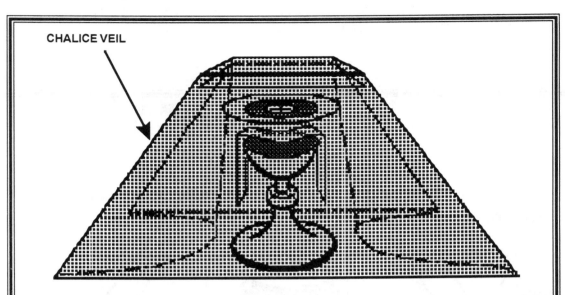

CHALICE VEIL

Fig. 6–5
Example of Veiled Chalice

Ensure that the edges of the veil are even in the front and the back and on each side. Some clergy prefer that the backside of the veil be folded back across the top, thereby leaving the backside of the chalice uncovered (and easier to pick up). This is another of those issues that you will need to check with your rector or vicar.

STEP 6 Put the corporal and two purificators in the burse and set it on top. (In some parishes, you will also place the key to the tabernacle or aumbry on top of the burse.)

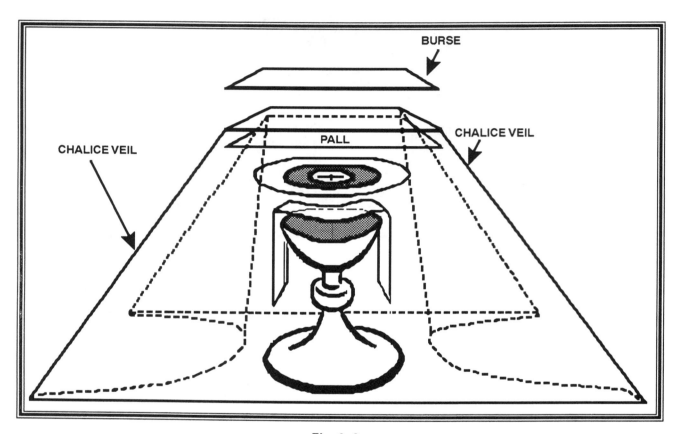

Fig. 6–6
Exploded View of Complete Chalice Set-up

Easy as all get out, isn't it?

SECOND CHALICE

If more than one chalice is needed, additional chalices are prepared in the same manner except:
- Do not include additional priest's wafers.
- Unless instructed to do so, do not place a paten on the second chalice.
- Do not veil additional chalices.
- No additional burse is required.

T.L.C. OF LINENS AND YOU

Whether you use the finest hand woven linen or wash-and- wear synthetics for altar linens, it in no way changes the tender loving care you give them – within reason.

An absolute necessity for any good altar guild is an electric teakettle. When the chalice (or chalices) are returned to the sacristy following the Eucharist, the purificators are usually in the chalice. Holding the chalice over the piscina, pour boiling water (from the teakettle) into the chalice (over the purificator).

Dropping the purificator(s) into the piscina, tilt the chalice sideways and turn it slowly as you continue to pour water from the teakettle. Doing this assures that all edges of the chalice are rinsed in boiling water and that the run-off, or excess water, flows over the purificators into the piscina.

Unfold and shake the purificators into the piscina. Check them for stains (i.e., wine, lipstick etc.). Treat any stains with soap or prewash stain remover, then place them in a basin of cold water until you are ready to wash them.

All of this ensures that proper disposition is made of any consecrated bread crumbs or wine that might remain in either chalice or purificator (because they are washed down the piscina). Also, it assures sterilization of the chalice(s) and prevents stains from setting in the fabric of the purificator(s).

LAUNDERING

Half the job of laundering the linens, especially the purificators, is in the care given immediately after a service. Prewash care saves wear and tear on both the altar guild and on the linens. Keep one (or several) of the prewash stain removers and a bar of Ivory soap on hand in the sacristy. These will save you from a lot of grief later.

It is not – repeat, is not – necessary or even desirable for all altar linens to be washed by hand. With modern washing machines that feature wide selections of water temperature and agitation speed, there is no longer any reason that fine altar linen cannot be machine washed. If nylon stockings, fine silk, and lace lingerie can be carefully machine washed, slow, gentle agitation and cool-to-warm water should be adequate to care for altar linen.

Of course, they must be laundered with great care. Drying altar linen in your home dryer should never be done. The heat from the dryer damages the linen more than washing ever could. To prepare the linens for easy ironing, remove them from the washer, arranging each piece flat on a large bath towel. Roll the towel from the bottom edge with the linen enclosed as you roll. Let the rolled towel sit for about thirty minutes before removing the linen, one piece at a time, as you iron them.

Some people prefer to dry linens in the sun and fresh air or spread flat on a covered counter or ironing board. That's fine, too, but the linen will have to be sprinkled and left to dampen evenly before ironing.

Laundering fair linen, unless you are blessed with a member or members who take on the task as a special thanksgiving, is sometimes best done by a reliable dry cleaner or commercial laundry. Because of its size, hand laundering is almost impossible. It can be laundered in the washer at home if it is put inside a mesh bag or a thin pillow slip. Otherwise it may get tied in knots or twisted in the washing machine, which can cause wear.

Never dry fair linen in a clothes dryer! Heat from the dryer will damage the fair linen.

IRONING
Ironing a fair linen is almost a two person or team effort, with one ironing and the other holding it straight or rolling it, as it is ironed, around a roller, "wrong" side to the roller so it will hang better when used. (Do not store fair linens folded.)

Once they are ironed and on a roller, wrap the fair linen in plastic and store it in a closet or cabinet with tightly fitting doors.

After careful laundering of the other linens, they may usually be ironed using a steam iron. Each piece, that is, corporal, purificator, lavabo and baptismal towel, has a particular way to be ironed.

Helpful Hint Number One:
If you dry the linens outside, or hang them up elsewhere, dampen and store them in a plastic bag in the refrigerator for a couple of hours before ironing.

Helpful Hint Number Two:
Iron with a steam iron while linens are still a little damp.

Helpful Hint Number Three:
Iron on the wrong side. (If you begin at any embroidered symbols, the area around the symbols will press out smoother.) Then fold and finger-press in folds on the right side. Your linens will look like new.

Ironing the Corporal

Iron the corporal flat, finishing with it right side up (see Figure 6–7a). Basically, you are going to fold it into nine equal squares. Ironing in the folds wears the linen. So, after ironing the corporal flat, simply finger-fold the top third toward you (see Figure 6–7b). The bottom third is finger-folded up and over the rest of the corporal (see Figure 6–7c). This makes it easy to find the cross and place it correctly on the altar. Finger-fold it in thirds again (see Figure 6–7d).

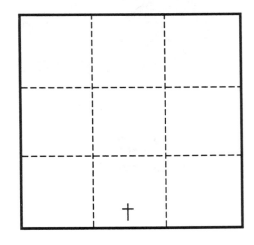

Fig. 6–7a
Iron Corporal Flat

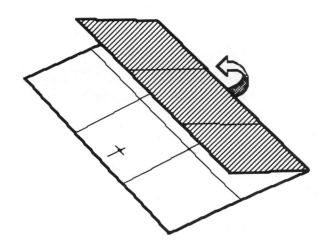

Fig. 6–7b
Finger-Fold Top Third Forward

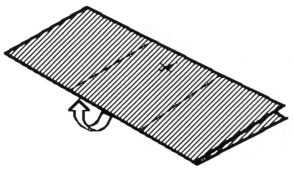

Fig. 6–7c
Finger-Fold Bottom Third
Up and Over

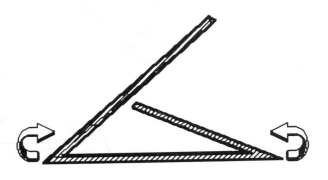

Fig. 6–7d
Finger-Fold in Thirds Again

Ironing the Purificator

This, too, is ironed and finger-folded into nine equal parts, right side to the outside, ending with the cross on top. Remember, ironing in the folds wears linen.

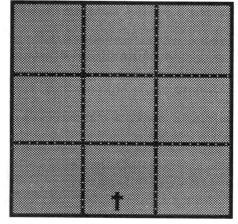

**Fig. 6–8a
Iron Purificator Flat
(with wrong side up)**

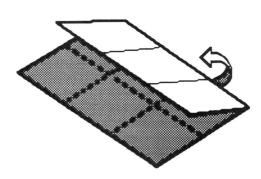

**Fig. 6–8b
Finger-Fold Top Third Forward
(right side outside)**

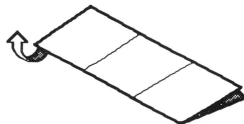

**Fig. 6–8c
Finger-Fold Bottom Third
Up and Over**

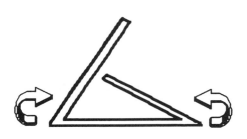

**Fig. 6–8d
Finger-Fold in Thirds Again**

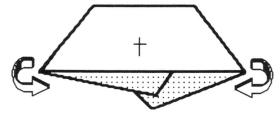

**Fig. 6–8e
Store with Cross on Top**

Ironing Lavabo and Baptismal Towels
Just fold into thirds lengthwise, the sides over the center, then in half.

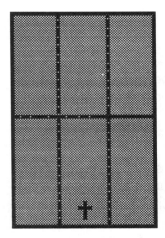

Fig. 6–9a
Iron Lavabo and Baptismal
Towels Flat

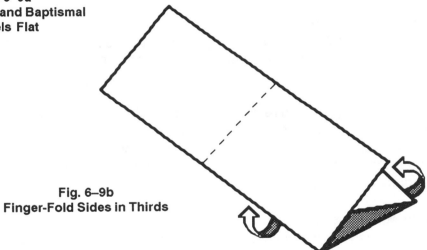

Fig. 6–9b
Finger-Fold Sides in Thirds

Fig. 6–9c
Finger-Fold in Half
and Store with Cross on Top

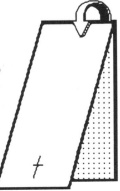

Ironing the Pall

The pall should be washed in soapy water, rinsed thoroughly, and placed on a water glass to dry. It requires no ironing.

STAIN REMOVAL

One of the major tasks undertaken by any altar guild member is how to get stains out of Yahweh's Yardgoods. Herewith we present some tried, if not true, techniques.

Removing Wine Stains

There are almost as many different ways of removing wine stains from purificators as there are types of purificators. They range from pouring boiling water through the stain while stretching it over a bowl, to rinsing briskly in cold water with or without rubbing the spot with salt, to spraying with a commercial prewash. Follow whatever procedures best work on the type of material for your "linens."

Removing Lipstick Stains

To remove lipstick stains, try soaking the spot in club soda for a while. Try using carbon tetachloride, *K2-R,* or *Unbelievable* prewash spray, or some other spot remover.

Hydrogen peroxide poured directly on the spot, rubbed and rinsed in cold water will remove blood stains, and it sometimes works on lipstick, too. The surest remedy is to post the following notice in the parish bulletin: "Those approaching the altar rail without having first removed their lipstick will automatically volunteer to do a month's worth of altar linen."

Removing Mildew

Use soap and water (run it through the washer again), rinse, then dry in the sun. If it's still there after rinsing, soak it in peroxide for about fifteen minutes. If that doesn't work, congratulations! You now have a new cleaning rag and the wrath of the altar guild director to face for letting it mildew in the first place.

Removing Rust

Wet the stain, sprinkle on salt, moisten with lemon juice, and dry in the sun. Rinse it with an ammonia-water solution, work in hot water and soap and dry in the sun again. (This means gradually add hot soap and water – it does not mean that you must be in hot, soapy water as you work.)

Removing Scorches
For a small, light scorch, dampen it with cool water and dry in the sun. Deep scorching destroys the fiber of the material, so anything badly scorched will have to be discarded.

Removing Oil, Grease, or Wax
Oil stains, grease, or candle wax are treated by scraping with a dull knife, soaking in a saucer of mild cleaning fluid for ten to twenty minutes, then washing in hot, soapy water. Prewash spot remover may also be used. Suppliers of religious articles offer wax removers through their catalogs.

General Reminders
Remember, any linen scorched beyond hope, ruined by mildew, or torn beyond mending should be burned and the ashes scattered on the earth or washed down the piscina. Or it may be deconsecrated for other use.

When washing small linens in a washer it may be helpful to put them in a small mesh bag.

Lavabo towels, corporals (unless spotted with wine), and credence cloths often need only rinsing, but to be on the safe side, wash them anyway.

SUMMARY
Linen is a general term used for the various cloths used, rather than an actual description of a type of material.

A *cerecloth* is a waxed linen the exact size of the altar slab that is used to cover the top of the altar. Its purpose is to protect the Fair Linen from dampness or stains. The use of a cerecloth is optional.

A *second linen* may be used lying on top of the cerecloth if needed for attaching superfrontals. The linen on top of the altar is called the "fair linen." It covers the entire top of the altar and may hang down over the ends to any length, even to the footpace. It is covered by a dust cover when the altar is not being used.

The *corporal* is a "placemat" to protect the fair linen and to catch any particles of the Blessed Sacrament or drops of wine which might fall on it during the Eucharist. A second, and more rigid, corporal placed over the chalice is called a *pall*.

Considerably smaller than a corporal, a purificator is used to clean the lip of the chalice as each person is communicated, and also to clean the chalice and paten during the ablutions.

The *lavabo towel* is folded and placed across the lavabo bowl to be used when the celebrant washes his or her fingers during the offertory. The *veil* matches the vestments worn by the celebrant and is a covering for the communion vessels. A *burse* is a case placed on top of the veiled communion vessels to hold the corporal and extra purificators. It matches the chalice veil.

To prepare for a Eucharist, place a purificator across the top of the chalice. Place the paten on top of these. Place the large, priest's wafer on the paten. Cover the paten with a pall. Drape all of these with the veil. Finally, place the corporal and a couple of purificators in the burse and set it on top.

It is not necessary for some altar linens to be washed by hand. However, they must be laundered with care, but that may be done in a washer, using cool water and gentle detergent. They should *never* be dried in a dryer.

Prewash care immediately after the service saves wear and tear on both the altar guild and on the linens.

Laundering fair linens is most often best done by a reliable dry cleaner or commercial laundry.

If you feel comfortable with the information contained in Module 6, proceed to the progress check. If not, you may wish to review the module again before completing the progress check.

MODULE 6
PROGRESS CHECK

Respond to the questions by filling in the blanks. Feel free to use the text of the module to assist you in answering.

1. Smaller than a corporal, a _____ is used to clean the lip of the chalice as each person is communicated.

2. A _____ is a case placed on top of the veiled communion vessels to hold the corporal and extra purificators.

3. _____ is a general term used for the various cloths used, rather than an actual description of a type of material.

4. The purpose of a _____ is to protect the fair linen from damp-ness that is characteristic of stone altars, or stains from wooden ones.

(ANSWERS ON THE BACK OF THIS SHEET)

MODULE 6
ANSWER SHEET

Respond to the questions by filling in the blanks. Feel free to use the text of the module to assist you in answering.

1. Smaller than a corporal, a **purificator** is used to clean the lip of the chalice as each person is communicated.

2. A **burse** is a case placed on top of the veiled communion vessels to hold the corporal and extra purificators.

3. **Linen** is a general term used for the various cloths used, rather than an actual description of a type of material.

4. The purpose of a **cerecloth** is to protect the fair linen from dampness that is characteristic of stone altars, or stains from wooden ones.

Now, look over your answers. If you feel comfortable that you understand the material in Module 6, please continue to Module 7. If not, you may wish to review the material again.

MODULE 7
VESTMENTS

*A play can really be boring with no costumes. The wardrobe –
and the wardrobe keepers – are critical to the successful performance. When an actor requires a wardrobe change in the
middle of Act II, and the costume change is missing. . . Well,
you get the idea.*

TIME:
Approximately 45 minutes

OBJECTIVE:
Given the contents of Module 7, you will be able to demonstrate an understanding of the types of vestments used in the American Episcopal Church by responding to simple fill-in-the-blank questions with 100% accuracy.

ACTIVITIES:
- Read the text of the module
- Complete Progress Check

MATERIAL REQUIRED:
- This Module
- Pen or Pencil
- Progress Check

OTHER RESOURCE MATERIAL:
None

COURSE MAP

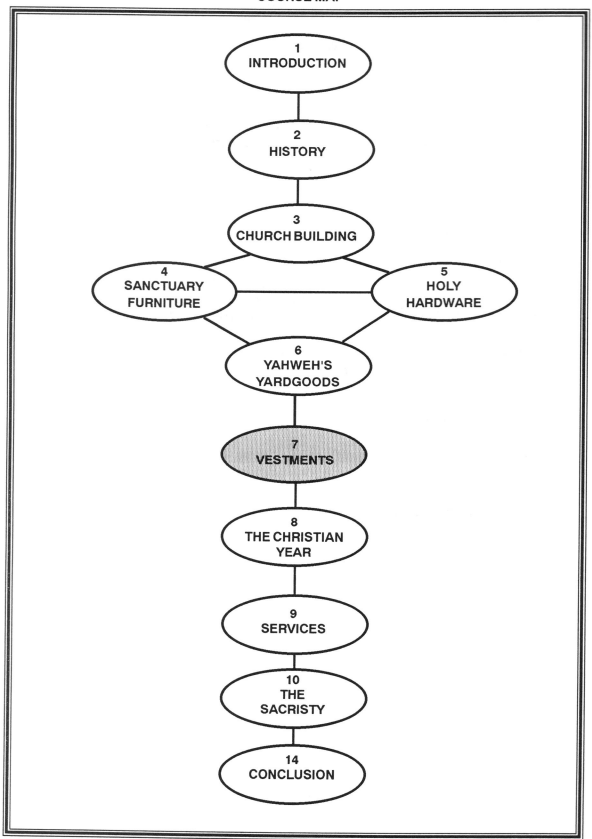

MODULE 7
VESTMENTS

INTRODUCTION

The ecclesiastical garments worn by the various orders of ministers in the performance of their duties are called vestments. They may, and usually do, vary according to the titles and duties of those who wear them.

Vestments evolved from the everyday clothing of the middle class during the late Roman Empire, and the clergy continued to wear them after fashion changed, down to this very day.

During this module we will discuss all kinds of vestments. But let's learn two new terms: 1) "Choir Vestments" (or "Choir Dress") and 2) "Eucharistic Vestments." Choir dress is a term used to describe the garments worn at all services other than Masses. Eucharistic vestments are vestments related to the celebration of the Holy Eucharist. Having made this distinction, we will now tell you that you will very seldom (if ever) hear the terms used. So, as we present the various vestments, we will arbitrarily present them to you in what we consider to be a logical order — and we will attempt to identify them as "choir" or "eucharistic" in nature.

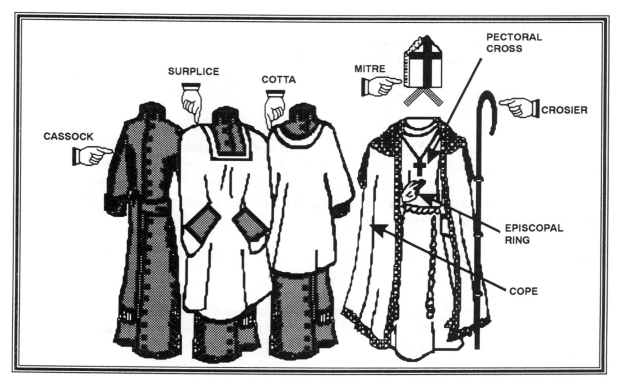

Fig. 7–1
Examples of "Choir Vestments"

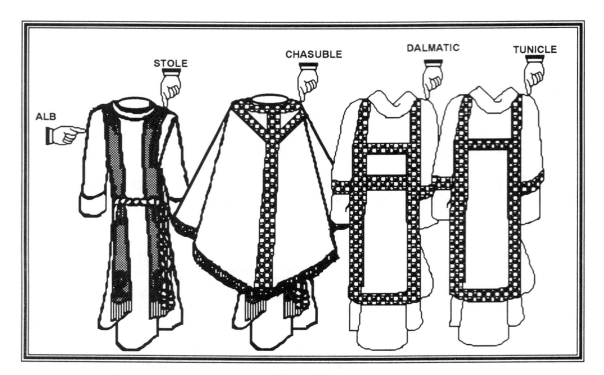

Fig. 7–2
Examples of "Eucharistic Vestments"

VESTMENT EVOLUTION

At first, vestments were very plain, but as time passed, they gradually were made of richer materials, decorated by needlework, appliques, and even jeweled. Additional vestments, such as the full, open-front type of chasuble called the "cope" evolved, as did special kinds of dress for bishops (i.e., the rochet, chimere, surplice, and mitre).

The use of vestments and the kind and type of vestment used vary widely — sometimes even wildly — from place to place in the American church and even within the same diocese. Unfortunately, the use of vestments is still, in some areas, the measure of the churchmanship of a parish. These are issues which should have been laid to rest ages ago.

The church, because of these differences, has tried (in the BCP) to set some guidelines for the minimum use of vestments.

The Book of Common Prayer, 1549, specifically stated that a celebrant was to wear a plain white alb with "vestment" (i.e., chasuble or cope) and that assisting clergy wear "albs with tunicles."

Following a very lively controversy, the 1552 revision merely states that deacons and priests wear surplices only, and that bishops wear rochets (a fancy surplice-like garment, usually adorned with lace and colored ribbons that tie a gathered collar). The book of 1559, the Elizabethan Book, contained an *Ornaments Rubric,* subject to varying interpretations. But in actual practice, from then until the late nineteenth century, normal dress was ankle-length surplices, black preaching gowns, and the occasional use of a cope.

Then eucharistic vestments came into vogue again in Anglicanism and are to this day. There has been a general return to the use of longer, fuller, more attractive prebaroque forms of vestments. Ornamentation is more creative, use of materials and color more imaginative. The alb and amice are often combined into one garment, as are the alb and cassock (the cassock-alb). The maniple, of no obvious significance, is seldom used. And, because of the modern designs of albs, the girdle is no longer always needed. The stole is often worn as an over stole – over rather than under the chasuble – thus providing for color variation and eliminating the need for a number of costly chasubles.

THE CASSOCK

The *cassock* (from the French *casaque,* for a type of jacket) is the basic dress of clergy, choir, and lay assistants, yet it is not considered a liturgical vestment. It is a long, skirted garment which reaches from shoulder to ankle, usually black, but varying according to the rank and duties of the wearer. A bishop's cassock may be either magenta or blue-violet, or black with magenta piping and buttons.

Ordinarily, a priest's cassock is black, unless he or she is a dean, archdeacon or canon, in which case the cassock is often trimmed with magenta piping and buttons.

Cincture

CINCTURE

A *cincture* (from the Latin *cinctura,* meaning 'a girdle') is a wide, cumberbund-like garment that is worn around the waist with two strips of material that hang from the top of the waistband. The color or piping of the cincture matches the cassock. It is not uncommon for the terms cincture and girdle to be used interchangeably.

Fig. 7–3
Example of Cassock with Cincture

SURPLICE

Lay readers, if vested, wear black cassocks and white *surplices*. Acolytes and choir cassocks, heretofore, usually black and worn with a surplice or cotta (a surplice-like garment, only shorter), may be of almost any color, worn with or without a cotta or surplice.

A *surplice* (from Middle English *surplis,* which was passed down from the Latin *superpelliceum,* meaning 'a fur robe made of skins') is a long, loose-sleeved garment made of white, lightweight material, worn over a cassock. It may vary in length anywhere from fingertip to almost ankle length.

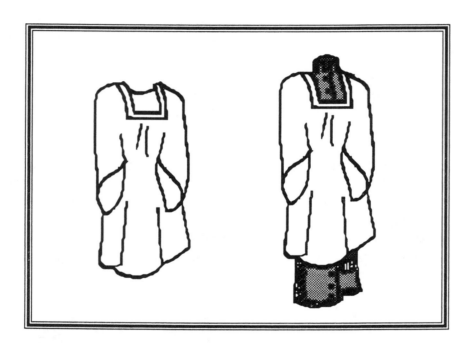

Fig. 7–4
Example of Surplice and Surplice Over Cassock

COTTA

Usually worn by acolytes, a *cotta* (from the Latin *kotta,* for 'coat') is the same as a surplice but shorter, and, whereas clergy surplices may be adorned by an embroidered cross, cottas are plain.

Fig. 7–5
Example of Cotta and Cotta Over Cassock

EUCHARISTIC VESTMENTS

Eucharistic vestments are those worn by priest or celebrant, deacon, and sub-deacon, if any, during the celebration of the Holy Eucharist. Even though some of the vestments are no longer used in some parishes, we will deal with all of them.

First though, remember from Module 6 (Linen) that in addition to the garments worn by the clergy, the burse and the veil which cover the chalice and paten are considered part of a "set" of eucharistic vestments and are made or bought to match the rest of the set.

The basic liturgical garment was, and is, the alb. It is long, full, and white. It may be worn over a cassock, or (as with a cassock-alb) alone, at the priest's discretion. Until resent times it was worn with an amice (a sort of neckpiece or collar), a girdle (a type of rope belt), and a maniple (an ecclesiastical napkin worn over the arm). The chasuble, dalmatic, and tunicle are all types of ecclesiastical coats. The stole (a long strip of cloth symbolizing and signifying the yoke of Christ) worn over the alb, was the distinctive mark of the bishop, priest, or deacon. It still is, no matter what else may be worn.

Fig. 7–6
Example of Alb with Girdle

ALB

The *alb* takes its name from the Latin *albus* meaning 'white.' Hence, it is a long, white garment that reaches to the hem of the cassock or the top of the shoe. In warmer climates the priest may elect not to wear a cassock under the alb, which is perfectly proper. Today, there are garments called cassock-albs which make the wearing of a cassock superfluous anyway.

Albs come in all styles, some of which have collars or hoods making the use of an amice unnecessary.

To clarify a point, an *amice* (from the Latin word *amictus,* meaning a 'cloak') was originally an oblong head covering, pushed back and worn around the neck like a collar. It is a large white, rectangular cloth with long strings attached to the top edges, which go around the waist and tie in front. Though in declining use, the amice still helps prevent "ring around the alb collar."

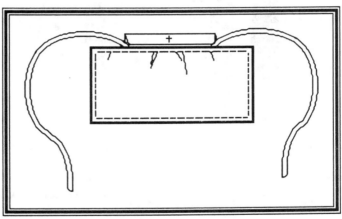

Fig. 7–7
Example of Amice

Some albs and amices have bands of silk, damask, or embroidery called apparels attached to the sleeves and skirt. These may change with season or occasion also.

STOLES

Stoles (from the Latin *stola,* for garment), in the color of the day or the occasion, are the badge of ordination worn over both shoulders hanging straight down in front by bishops and priests; over the left shoulder and tied (or otherwise joined) under the right arm by deacons.

Fig. 7–8a
Example of Priest's Stole Worn
Over Alb

Fig. 7–8b
Example of Deacon's Stole
Worn Over Left Shoulder

A shorter matching stole called a *preaching stole* may be worn by the preacher when only delivering the Liturgy of the Word and not functioning in the Eucharist – other than to assist with communion. It is worn over a cassock and surplice, cassock-alb, or alb.

Today, the stole is often worn over rather than under the chasuble, in which case it is usually of a wider design, and is called an *outer stole* or *over stole*. Its use can provide for variations in color without the costly outlay for a number of different chasubles in liturgical colors.

Deacons also wear stoles as a badge of their ordination. The deacon's stole is worn over the left shoulder and either looped or tied on the right side, just below the cincture. Many vestment sets include a separate deacon's stole that has some type of connector (i.e., frog, snap, strap, etc.) for joining the two lower ends of the stole.

THE CHASUBLE

The *chasuble* (from medieval Latin *casubula,* for 'little cottage') is a one-piece garment, open on the sides with an opening for the head, and worn by a priest and/or bishop for the celebration of the Eucharist. It can be worn in procession under the cope, but general practice is that it be placed over the altar rail or in some easily accessible place so that the celebrant may be vested at the offertory.

The *chasuble* is the most distinctive of all the eucharistic vestments. Its origins are in the enveloping cloak worn by everyone at the time of Christ. Worn over alb and stole, unless an outer stole is used, it is thought to symbolize Christian Charity.

This garment, not unlike the others, has undergone considerable metamorphosis, from full-cut to the medieval skimpy "Fiddle Back" to the conical (Heaven help the priest who forgot and dropped both arms at the same time!), up to the recent trend toward the return of the more attractive, fuller-cut Byzantine style.

Fig. 7–9
Example of Chasuble

THE DALMATIC

A *dalmatic* (from Lower Latin *dalmatica,* because originally they were made of Dalmatian wool) is worn by the deacon at a Eucharist or Solemn Mass. It is worn over the alb and deacon's stole. (This is true even when the "deacon" at Mass is a priest. The dalmatic matches the rest of the vestments in color, trim, and style, but has sleeves, which the chasuble does not. The dalmatic is usually more ornamental than its matching tunicle, worn by the subdeacon.

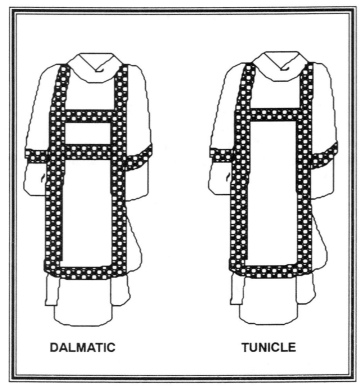

DALMATIC   **TUNICLE**

Fig. 7–10
Examples of Dalmatic and Tunicle

THE TUNICLE

Exactly like the dalmatic, the *tunicle* (from the Latin *tunicula,* the diminutive of the common Roman *tunic*) matches the rest of the eucharistic vestments but with less ornamentation. If the dalmatic has two "bars" or rows of trim, the tunicle has one. The subdeacon who wears the tunicle does not wear a stole. Hence, function dictates dress. The subdeacon at a Solmn High Mass may be a bishop, but at this Mass he or she is functioning as a subdeacon, and therefore wears no visible signs of office – save perhaps for an episcopal ring.

COPE

A *cope* (from medieval Latin *capa,* and Latin *caput,* meaning 'head') is a choir vestment of dignity which may be worn by any order of the clergy. It is a long semicircular cloak of rich material generally matching other vestments in the color of the season.

(As an altar guild member, please do everything in your power to see that the cope is of a good shoe-top length. Nothing presents more ludicrous a spectacle than a person in a ballerina-length cope or one which drags two feet behind like a bridal train, although the latter is preferable.)

A cope may be worn over an alb or surplice for solemn processions, benedictions, funerals, weddings, matins, or evensong. (Matins and evensong are daily offices that will be covered in a later module.)

Fig. 7–11
Example of Cope

OTHER VESTMENTS

There are other items which fall into the category of vestments that may or may not be in use in your parish. A brief description of these and their usage is included here.

The Humeral Veil

A *humeral veil* is a large, wide scarf (considered a eucharistic vestment) worn around the priest's shoulders and down both arms (and hands), as a protective veil in carrying the Blessed Sacrament (especially in the monstrance) from one place to another inside the church. It is used at Solemn Benediction of the Blessed Sacrament and sometimes in the procession to the Altar of Repose on Maundy Thursday.

Tippet

A *tippet* (considered a choir vestment) is a wide black scarf sometimes worn over a surplice for the choir offices. Some clergy ornament them with the shields of their seminaries or the diocese. They are sometimes worn by the preacher at the offices, also.

Academic Hood

The *academic hood* (also a choir vestment) is worn to signify a college degree, usually the highest one possesses. It may be worn during choir offices over cassock and surplice. The shape, size, and color denotes the type of degree, and the granting college institution or university.

THE BISHOP'S CHOIR DRESS

The choir vestments of a bishop are also badges of episcopal power and office and are considered a part of the bishop's regalia. Cassocks and other wardrobe worn by a bishop are usually magenta or blue-violet, or black with magenta piping and buttons. In addition a bishop wears:

The Pectoral Cross

A *pectoral cross* is a large cross, usually of precious metal worn around the neck and upon the chest. Its use is not limited to a bishop. Historically the bishop's pectoral cross contained a relic of a martyr symbolizing the power of the cross through the sufferings of the faithful.

**Fig. 7–12
Examples Pectoral Crosses
Worn with Cassock and Alb**

The Episcopal Ring

The *episcopal ring* is the symbol of the bishop's authority and is usually worn on the third finger of the right hand. Usually made of gold and set with an amethyst, it represents the bishop's betrothal to the church.

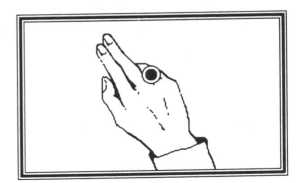

**Fig. 7–13
Example of Episcopal Ring**

The Crosier or Pastoral Staff

The long walking staff or shepherd's crook carried by or in front of a bishop in the home diocese is called a *crosier* (from the Old French *crossier,* meaning 'the one bearing the cross'). It is a symbol of the bishop as shepherd to Christ's flock.

Crosiers are sometimes made of wood or brass. Rarely today are they made of gold or silver. Many modern crosier's are designed to collapse. Our son, who often served as the bishop's server, called it "the bishop's portable God-rod."

When the crosier is carried with the crook pointing in the same direction as the bishop faces, it is a symbol that the bishop is a "diocesan bishop." When the crook points backward (or toward the bishop's shoulder), it is a symbol that the bishop is a *co-adjutor* or *suffragan* bishop. A co-adjutor bishop automatically becomes diocesan bishop on the retirement, resignation, or death of the diocesan bishop. A suffragan bishop does not.

(A long-standing joke on the matter is that a suffragan bishop comes into the diocesan bishop's office every morning and says, "Good morning, Bishop!" The co-adjutor comes in and asks, "How are you feeling this morning, Bishop?")

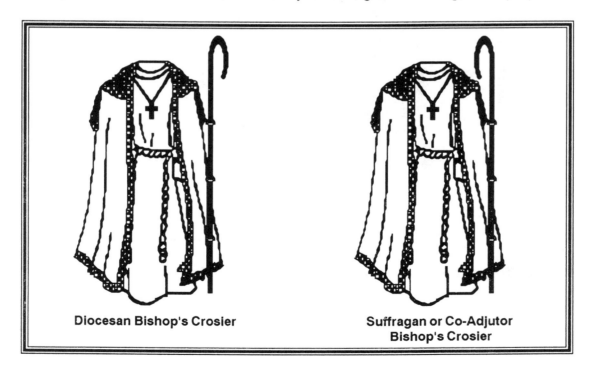

Diocesan Bishop's Crosier   Suffragan or Co-Adjutor
                                    Bishop's Crosier

Fig. 7–14
Examples of
Bishop's Crosier

The Mitre

A bishop's *mitre* (from the Latin *mitra,* meaning 'cap') is the official "hat" of the bishop worn whenever performing a definitely episcopal act. It is the most conspicuous of the choir dress of a bishop. The mitre is worn when in procession, at confirmations, ordinations, and when giving a blessing. Its shape is symbolic of the Holy Spirit, who descended in the form of tongues of fire coming to rest on the heads of the apostles on the day of Pentecost.

The two tails hanging down from the back of the mitre look like book marks because that is what they are there to symbolize. At some consecrations a Gospel book is placed on the new bishop's head as an indication of the message that he or she is to proclaim. The mitre is removed when the bishop either hears the Gospel or prays. Therefore, after a procession, the bishop usually will remove the mitre during the Liturgy of the Word and will not put it back on until after communion, for the final blessing.

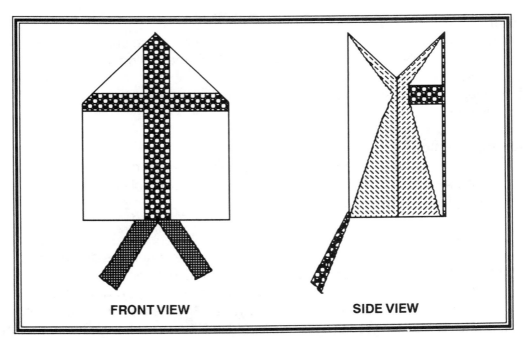

FRONT VIEW   SIDE VIEW

Fig. 7–15
Front and Side Examples of
Bishop's Mitre

The Rochet

A *rochet* (from Middle English *roc,* meaning 'a cloak') is a kind of surplice worn by a bishop. It may be a long, full-length, surplice-type with full sleeves gathered at the wrist and worn under a *chimere* (a long black or magenta sleeveless coat-type gown that is open down the front). Or, a rochet may be of plain sleeves worn over a cassock, without chimere.

MISCELLANEOUS MISCHIEF
There are some additional cloth-type things that do not really fall under any of the categories discussed to this point. Rather than confirm an old altar guild suspicion (that they are there strictly for the busy-work of the altar guild), we will cover them here.

Pulpit or Lectern Falls
Pulpit or *lectern falls* are also called *antependia*. In some churches they are hung over the front of the pulpit or lectern (or both). Pulpit/lectern falls usually come in seasonal colors and with seasonal ornamentation – church seasons, that is. (Seasons will be covered in the next module.)

Bible Markers
Just what the name implies, *Bible markers* are wide ribbons in the color of the day used to mark the Bible citations or proper for the day.

Banners
The design and use of *banners* is limited only by the artistic imagination and ingenuity of their creators. They may be hung from the ceiling or walls, or carried in procession. No church should be without its official banner. Seasonal banners and banners for special occasions add to the color and excitement of the worship of Almighty God.

Wedding Cushions
Wedding cushions are placed on the altar step for the use of the bride and groom when they kneel. They usually have wedding symbols on them and are sometimes, but not always, white.

The Funeral Pall
The *funeral pall* is the covering placed over the casket when the deceased is brought into the church for service of Christian burial, whether Requiem Mass or simple Burial Office. Since black is no longer considered appropriate for Christian burial, and since the funeral rite in the Prayer Book is an Easter liturgy in thanksgiving for our own resurrection with and in Christ and for the life of the one who has died, white with gold or some other color is now used for funeral palls and for all other vestments of the funeral service.

The funeral pall has another symbolism. Death is the great equalizer. We are all the same in the eyes of God. Therefore, it matters not if the casket containing the mortal remains be of hammered bronze or flannel-covered particle board, we are all enveloped by God's love. That's what the pall reminds us.

Further, flowers other than those at the altar, are NEVER – repeat NEVER – allowed in the church at a funeral. If the casket arrives covered with a floral casket cover the flowers are removed and left either outside or in the narthex. It may be replaced once the funeral pall is removed, after the funeral.

The funeral pall should be large enough to cover the casket entirely, approximately seven feet by eleven feet. However, since the casket rides on a contraption called a "church truck," a pall slightly larger – eight feet by twelve feet – will extend to the floor and looks nicer. Most funeral directors can be taught how to tuck it up to keep it out of the way of the church truck's wheels.

A white veil or other appropriate covering should be available for an urn containing ashes from cremation (cremains).

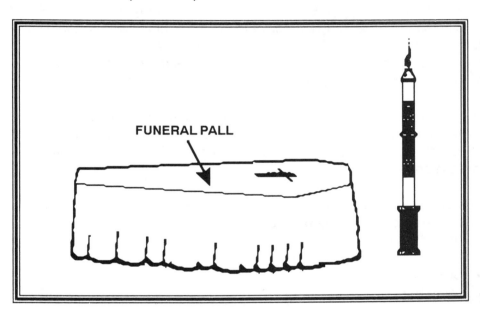

FUNERAL PALL

Fig. 7–16
Example of Funeral Pall

SUMMARY

Ecclesiastical garments worn by the various orders of ministers in the performance of their duties are called vestments. They vary according to the titles and duties of those who wear them.

Choir vestments is a term used to describe the garments worn at all services other than Masses (celebrations of the Eucharist).

Early vestments were very plain, but gradually became more elaborate. Today there is a general return to the use of longer, fuller, more attractive forms of vestments. The alb and amice are often combined into one garment, as are the alb and cassock (the cassock-alb).

The cassock is the basic dress of clergy, choir, and lay assistants. A bishop's cassock may be either magenta or blue-violet, or black with magenta piping and buttons. Ordinarily a priest's cassock is black. Lay readers wear black cassocks and white surplices. Acolyte and choir cassocks may be of almost any color, worn with or without a cotta or surplice.

A surplice is a long, loose-sleeved garment made of white, lightweight material, worn over a cassock. It may vary in length anywhere from fingertip to almost ankle length. Cottas are the same but shorter. A full open-front type of chasuble is called a *cope*.

The Choir vestments of a bishop are badges of episcopal power and office and are considered a part of the bishop's regalia. These include:
- A pectoral cross
- An episcopal ring
- A crosier
- A rochet
- A mitre

Eucharistic vestments are those worn by priest or celebrant, deacon, and sub-deacon, if any, during the celebration of the Holy Eucharist. The burse and the veil are considered part of a set of vestments.

The basic liturgical garment is the alb. Sometimes it is still worn with an amice, a girdle, and a maniple. The chasuble, dalmatic, and tunicle are all types of ecclesiastical coats. The stole, worn over the alb, is the distinctive mark of the bishop, priest, or deacon.

The word *alb* comes from the Latin *albus* meaning 'white.' Hence it is a long, white garment that reaches to the hem of the cassock or the top of the shoe. An *amice* was originally a head covering, pushed back and worn around the neck like a collar. It is a large, white, rectangular cloth with long strings attached to the top edges, which go around the waist and tie in front.

Stoles are the badge of ordination worn over both shoulders hanging straight down in front by bishops or priests and over the left shoulder by deacons. The *chasuble* is a one piece garment, open on the sides with an opening for the head and worn by priest and/or bishop for the celebration of the Eucharist. The *dalmatic* is worn by the deacon at a Eucharist over the alb and a stole. The *tunicle* is exactly like the dalmatic, but with less ornamentation.

The *humeral veil* is a large wide scarf worn around the priest's shoulders as a protective veil in carrying the Blessed Sacrament from one place to another inside the church. *Pulpit* or *lectern falls* are hung over the front of the pulpit or the lectern (or both). *Bible markers* are wide ribbons in the color of the day used to mark the Bible citations or proper for the day. *Banners* may be hung from the ceiling or walls, or carried in procession. Seasonal banners and banners for special occasions add to the color and excitement of worship.

Wedding cushions are placed on the altar step for the use of the bride and the groom when they kneel. They usually have wedding symbols on them and most of the time, but not always, are white. The *funeral pall* is the covering placed over the casket when the deceased is brought into the church for the burial office. A white veil or other appropriate covering should be available for an urn containing ashes from cremation (cremains).

If you feel comfortable with the information contained in Module 7, proceed to the progress check. If not, you may wish to review the module again before completing the progress check.

Special Note:
If it is required for a member of the Altar Guild to enter the Sanctuary when people are present in the nave, they should be "vested."
Placing (or removing) vessels, lighting (or extinguishing) candles or any other activity should be done in alb or cassock.

MODULE 7
PROGRESS CHECK

Respond to the questions by filling in the blanks. Feel free to use the text of the module to assist you in answering.

1. The _____ is the basic dress of clergy, choir, and lay assistants.

2. _____ _____ is a term used to describe the garments worn at all services other than Masses.

3. A _____ is the official "hat" of a bishop worn when performing an episcopal act.

4. The shepherd's crook carried by a bishop is called a_____.

5. Eucharistic vestments are worn by_____, _____, and_____ during the Holy Eucharist.

6. _____ are the badge of ordination worn over both shoulders hanging straight down in front by bishops or priests and over the left shoulder by deacons.

7. The basic liturgical garment is the_____.

8. The_____ is a one-piece garment, open on the sides with an opening for the head and worn by priest and/or bishop for the celebration of the_____.

(ANSWERS ON THE BACK OF THIS PAGE)

MODULE 7
ANSWER SHEET

Respond to the questions by filling in the blanks. Feel free to use the text of the module to assist you in answering.

1. The **cassock** is the basic dress of clergy, choir, and lay assistants.

2. **Choir vestments (choir dress)** is a term used to describe the garments worn at all services other than Masses.

3. A **mitre** is the official "hat" of a bishop worn when performing an episcopal act.

4. The shepherd's crook carried by a bishop is called a **crosier**.

5. Eucharistic vestments are worn by **priest (celebrant), deacon** and **subdeacon** during the Holy Eucharist.

6. **Stoles** are the badge of ordination worn over both shoulders hanging straight down in front by bishops or priests and over the left shoulder by deacons.

7. The basic liturgical garment is the **alb**.

8. The **chasuble** is a one piece garment, open on the sides with an opening for the head and worn by priest and/or bishop for the celebration of the **Eucharist**.

Now, look over your answers. If you feel comfortable that you understand the material in Module 7, please continue to Module 8. If not, you may wish to review the material again.

MODULE 8
THE CHRISTIAN YEAR

Theater groups post their "season" (the list and schedule of plays that will be performed during the show season). Well, we have been doing the same play for a long time; and we continue to "do" it season after season, but we use different costumes and sometimes different props. Backstage, we need to know which performance of our basic passion play is on stage at all times.

TIME:
Approximately 30 minutes

OBJECTIVE:
Given the contents of Module 8, you will be able to demonstrate an understanding of the church year including (1) how the year is divided (2) the various seasons of the church year, (3) how to determine movable dates of feasts and holy days, and (4) assigned and optional colors used during the church year, by responding to simple fill-in-the-blank questions with 100% accuracy.

ACTIVITIES:
- Read the text of the module
- Complete Progress Check

MATERIAL REQUIRED:
- This Module
- Pen or Pencil
- Progress Check

OTHER RESOURCE MATERIAL:
Book of Common Prayer
Ordo Calendar

COURSE MAP

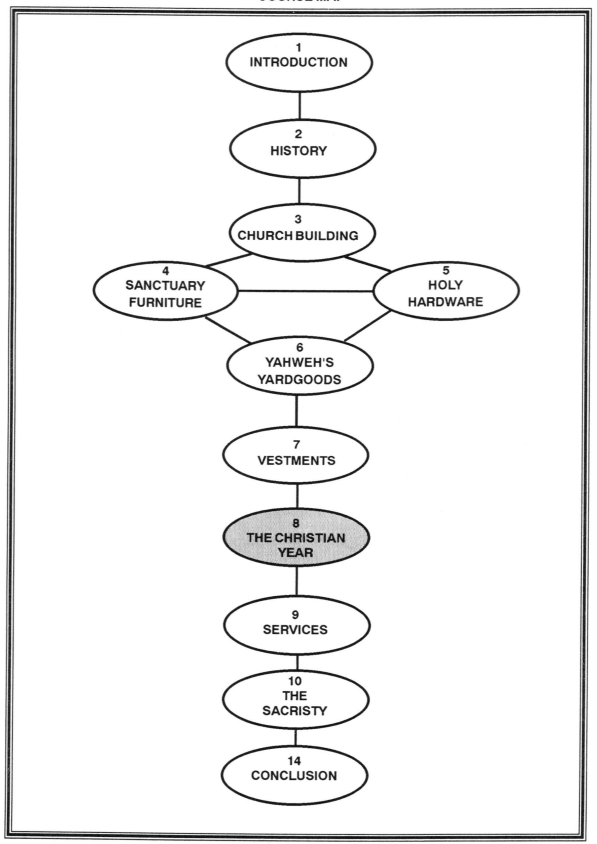

MODULE 8
THE CHRISTIAN YEAR

INTRODUCTION

The calendar of the church year, found on page 15 of the Book of Common Prayer, is not as hopelessly confusing as first glance might have us believe. To the uninitiate – and that includes some life-long Episcopalians who have never taken the time to study it – this section may make us feel that we have stumbled upon something only a bit less confusing than the Rosetta Stone, untranslated, or Einstein's Theory of Relativity.

But take heart! That really isn't the case at all. Besides, no one is expected to remember when the church celebrates the Feast of Saint Polycarp. We have wonderful tools called "Ordo Calendars" which keep track of all those wondrous things for us – up to a point. And, of course, each season has its corresponding symbolic color, more or less. But we will deal with that separately.

APRIL

S	M	T	W	T	F	S
26 (White)	27 (White)	28 (White)	29 (White)	30 (White)	31 (White)	1 (White)
2 (White)	3 St. Joseph (transferred) (White)	4 Annunciation of Our Lord (transferred) (White)	5 (White)	6 (White)	7 (White)	8 (White)
9 (White)	10 (White)	11 (White)	12 (White)	13 (White)	14 (White)	15 (White)
16 (White)	17 (White)	18 (White)	19 (White)	20 (White)	21 (White)	22 (White)
23 (White)	24 (White)	25 Saint Mark (Red)	26 (White)	27 (White)	28 (White)	29 (White)
30 (White)	1 St. Philip and St. James, Apostles (Red)	2 (White)	3 (White)	4 (White)	5 (White)	6 (White)

Fig. 8–1
Example of Ordo Calendar

With an Ordo (from the Latin *ordo,* meaning ' a regular series') Calendar, all you need to do is look. Chances are there is an Ordo Calendar posted in your sacristy. A good (but unofficial) exercise would be for you to check during your next pass through. But what if you don't have an Ordo Calendar handy? It is important for you to be able to determine where you are (in relation to the church year), even without the help of "Saint Ordo."

For now, let's look at the church year as it is observed and celebrated according to the 1979 Book of Common Prayer, and the Book of Occasional Services. For a detailed study of the church calendar, how it came to be, and how it has been expanded and changed down through the centuries, we recommend reading the *Commentary on the American Prayer Book* by Marion J. Hatchett, published by Harper and Row (formerly Seabury Press).

Perhaps it is an oversimplification to say that the church year is a Christian year and proclaims, at all times, the *mysterium Christi* (the mystery of Christ). Yet it is neither a review of the entirety of salvation history, nor is it, in its observance, a comprehensive study course in all the doctrine of the faith. Still it doesn't hurt.

THE SEVEN-DAY WEEK

The basic framework upon which the church year is structured is the seven-day cycle or seven-day week with Sunday, the Lord's Day (the day of the resurrection) being counted as the first day. Further, the Great Fifty Days, from Easter to Pentecost, divides the year roughly into two periods: one represents Christ in his earthly life; the other presents his reigning life through the Holy Spirit in his church until his coming again.

THE SEASONS

The church seasons are Advent, Christmas, Epiphany, Lent, Easter, and the season after Pentecost. The present Book of Common Prayer with proper prefaces for each Lord's Day stressing Sunday as the day of creation, resurrection, and the outpouring of the Holy Spirit, gives precedence to the celebration of Sundays over saints' days, thus attempting to restore the primacy of Sunday within the liturgical week. Each Sunday, is, in fact, a "little Easter."

To begin the study, first of all, turn to page 15 in *your* copy of the 1979 Book of Common Prayer.

Locate and underline the following (that's the reason it should be your own personal copy):

The Church Year consists of two cycles of feasts and holy days: one is dependent upon the movable date of the Sunday of the Resurrection or Easter Day; the other, upon the fixed date of December 25, the Feast of our Lord's Nativity or Christmas Day.

Easter Day is always the first Sunday after the full moon that falls on or after March 21. [Thus, according to Lunar Cycle:] **It cannot occur before March 22 or after April 25.**

Why? I hear you ask. Because it can't! That's the way the solar system works! Now flip to page 882 in the BCP. There, and on the next page, you will see *A Table to Find Easter Day* (from 1900 through 2089).

Once you know the date of Easter, you can turn the page (to page 884) and find another *Table to Find Movable Feasts and Holy Days*.

Easter Day	Sundays after Epiphany*	Ash Wednesday	Ascension Day	Pentecost	Numbered Proper of 2 Pentecost	Advent Sunday
March 22	4	Feb. 4	April 30	May 10	#3	November 29
March 23	4	Feb. 5	May 1	May 11	#3	November 30
March 24	4	Feb. 6	May 2	May 12	#3	December 1
March 25	5	Feb. 7	May 3	May 13	#3	December 2
March 26	5	Feb. 8	May 4	May 14	#3	December 3
March 27	5	Feb. 9	May 5	May 15	#4	November 27
(chart continues)						

Fig. 8–2
Partial copy of the 'Table to Find Movable Feasts and Holy Days'
from the BCP

For example, if Easter is on March 22, by following the chart across the page, you will see that:
- there are four Sundays after Epiphany;
- Ash Wednesday is on February 4;
- Ascension Day (always forty days after Easter and always on a Thursday) is April 30;
- Pentecost falls on May 10;
- Proper 3 is to be used on the Sunday after Trinity Sunday and from then on propers are used consecutively.
- Advent begins on November 29. (Advent always begins on the Sunday nearest the Feast of St. Andrew, November 30.)

EXERCISE 8–1
USING THE BCP TO FIND FEAST DAYS

Now that you see how it can be done, let's practice! The following exercise is designed to take you step-by-step through determining feast days.

1. First, looking at the **Table to Find Easter Day** (page 882), find the date for Easter Day in 1992. Easter Day, 1992 was: _____.

2. Notice that there is an asterisk (*) after the year 1992. Why?
    All years in the chart with an asterisk after them are _____
    _____.

3. Take your answer to question 1, and turn to the **Table to Find Movable Feasts and Holy Days** (pages 884-885). Using your date answer the following questions:

    3a. There were _____ Sundays after Epiphany.

    3b. Ash Wednesday was on _____.

    3c. Ascension Day was on _____.

    3d. Pentecost fell on _____.

    3e. The proper that was used on the Sunday after Trinity Sunday was Proper _____.

    3f. Advent Sunday fell on _____.

ANSWERS:

1.   April 19
2.   Leap Years
3a. 8
3b. March 4
3c. May 28
3d. June 7
3e. 7
3f. November 29

See, it's really not that complicated. Simply determine the date of Easter, then use the Movable Feasts Table to find the other dates.

ADVENT SEASON

The First Sunday of Advent was once described by a young man in an inquirers' class as "the church's own New Year's Day." And, really, it is. The church year begins with the First Sunday of Advent, always four Sundays before Christmas Day and the Sunday on or nearest Saint Andrew's Day, November 30. Advent ends with Midnight Mass on Christmas Eve.

Advent, taken from the Latin *adventus* (coming), is a season of preparation not only for Christmas, but also for the Second Coming of Christ at the last day. While it is a time of penitence marked by special devotion, it is not a "little Lent." The whole atmosphere of Advent should be quiet, joyful expectation and preparatory anticipation, mixed with penitence.

Fig. 8–3
Advent Wreath

Special altar guild preparations during Advent may include making (or providing) an *Advent wreath.* The wreaths take many forms, but usually feature three purple candles and a single pink candle – and occasionally include single white candle in the center.

CHRISTMAS

This season begins with the first Mass on Christmas Eve, December 24, and continues through twelve days of Christmas until January 6, the Feast of the Epiphany.

As we shall see, Constantine's legalization of Christianity early in the fourth century, about A.D. 320, had a tremendous effect on the development of the liturgical year. The feasts of Christmas and Epiphany developed as a means to Christianize *Saturnalia* , a pagan festival related to the winter solstice. Probably by the year A.D. 336, Christians had begun to celebrate December 25 as the feast day of the Incarnation – Almighty God taking on human flesh and coming among us.

Fig. 8–4
God in Human Flesh

Christmas has become such a favorite time of the year for Christians and non-Christians alike that all kinds of folklore and customs have grown up around it. For some altar guilds, in some churches, it has become a time of incredible "busy-ness." It is not uncommon for the sacristy, on the last days of Advent, to become less a place of holy preparation and more a chamber of ecclesiastical horrors.

This unfortunately seems true of Holy Week and Easter, too. With careful organization and utilization of time and talents, such need not, and *should* not, be the case. Do not let the "Grinch" steal your Christmas — nor let the image of Christ be lost in your spiritual, as well as physical, preparations for this holy day.

EPIPHANY

Epiphany comes on the twelfth day of Christmas, January 6, and is also known as "Twelfth Night." (Remembering the song *"The Twelve Days of Christmas"* might be helpful.) It is the season which commemorates the manifestation or "showing forth" of Christ to the Gentiles. It was on this day that the Wise Men (or *"Magi"*) – all Gentiles, incidentally – came to wor-

Fig. 8–5
Example of Christmas Banner

ship the Christ Child after following the star to his birthplace.

The First Sunday after the Epiphany is celebrated as the Feast of the Baptism of Our Lord, and is one of the four days especially appropriate for Holy Baptism (the others being the Easter Vigil, Pentecost, and All Saints').

The last day of Epiphany is Shrove Tuesday, so called from the ancient custom of going to the priest to be *shriven* (stripped) of one's sins by making confession and receiving absolution before beginning Lent the next day, Ash Wednesday.

Fig. 8–6
Epiphany Celebrates the Magi Coming to Worship

ASH WEDNESDAY

Ash Wednesday marks the beginning of the Lenten Season. The day takes its name from the ceremony of the imposition of ashes on the foreheads of the faithful with the words, "Remember that you are dust, and to dust you shall return." Psalm 103 appointed for the day is a *paean* (exalted song) of praise to God who forgives our sins and remembers that we are but dust. Dust bound for glory in Christ; forgiven dust; but mortal dust, none the less.

Ashes used on this day are obtained by burning palms and palm crosses left from the previous Palm Sunday. These can either be saved by the Altar Guild from left-over palms from the previous year, or returned by members of the congregation.

Fig. 8–7
Example of "Imposition of Ashes"

LENT

The season of Lent is comprised of the forty days before Easter, not counting the Sundays. It is roughly a tithe (10%) of the year, marked by solemn penitence and fasting. It grew out of a period of intense preparation through instruction, prayer, and fasting of baptismal candidates in the early church in preparation for baptism at the Easter Vigil. On page 265 of the BCP, all the faithful are urged to the keeping "holy Lent, by self-examination and repentance; by prayer, fasting and self-denial; and by reading and meditating on God's Holy Word." (The ten petitions in the Litany of Penitence (pp. 267-269) are a good basis for self-examination.) ·

Most parishes and missions provide extra services, various study groups and seminars, inter-age study programs for families, or other opportunities for spiritual growth during this time. *The Book of Occasional Services* contains Stations of the Cross, the "Way of the Cross," for Fridays in Lent (pp.55-71), and *Lesser Feasts and Fasts* includes proper collects and lessons for the weekdays in Lent (pp. 19-53)

Now, as members of the altar guild, you have no doubt already sensed increased time will have to be spent in the sacristy in preparation for these observances. You are right. But perhaps you might consider it a part of your own Lenten observance and discipline.

Fig. 8–8
Stations of the Cross

HOLY WEEK

Holy Week, the final week of Lent, begins on the Sunday of the Passion (Palm Sunday), and extends to the Eucharist concluding the Easter Vigil. Holy Week is the liturgical reenactment of the events in the last week of the earthly life of our Lord.

We are there with him (through the liturgy beginning on page 270 in the Prayer Book) from the *"Hosannas"* and *"Blessed is He who comes in the name of the Lord,"* at his triumphal entry into Jerusalem; through the trial before Caesar with its frightening display of mob violence and the cries of *"Crucify him! Crucify him!"*

We hear the echoes of the *Suffering Servant Songs* of Isaiah in our minds as we watch the travesty of a trial and all that follows. Our hearts ache as the Lord is stripped and scourged and whipped and made to carry the horrible instrument of his own death on his torn and bleeding back through the streets to Calvary. And we are there at the foot of his Cross when he says, *"Forgive them, for they know not what they do."* And we know he means *us,* too.

Maundy Thursday

But we are also there on Maundy Thursday when the Lord celebrates his Last Supper with the apostles. A devout young Jew, He took the bread and wine of the traditional *Chaburah* meal and forever changed its meaning by saying, "This is my body. . . This is my blood." And he gave a new commandment: *"Love one another as I have loved you. Peace is my last gift to you, my own peace I now leave with you; peace which the world cannot give, I give to you."*

The Maundy Thursday service, which departs from the dark colors of Lent, is usually celebrated with flowers and glorias, in contrast to the stark penitential atmosphere of the rest of Lent. It is followed, in most churches, by a procession to the Altar of Repose, the ritual stripping of the altar and sanctuary, and, in many places, a "prayer watch" by members of the congregation until the Good Friday observance.

Good Friday

Good Friday is the most solemn of all days in the Christian calendar. It is a day of deepest mourning marked with special services and observances which vary from parish to parish, with many, if not most, places now following the liturgy for Good Friday provided on page 276 in the Prayer Book.

In places where the Mass of the Presanctified is observed, Holy Communion is administered from the Reserved Sacrament, since there should be no Sacrament present in the church from Good Friday until the Mass of the Easter Vigil when the supply is replenished. The crosses are usually veiled in black or dark red and the tabernacle door is left open. The processions are silent.

Holy Saturday

No Eucharist is celebrated on Holy Saturday. The liturgy is one of quiet hope and anticipation. However, this is certainly a busy day for the Altar Guild. As we will discuss in the next module, the day is spent in multi-task preparations for Easter Day.

The paschal candle which is lighted from the "new fire" at the beginning of this service represents and symbolizes the risen Christ, the Light of the World, and is carried in solemn procession through a darkened church to the sanctuary where it stands and is lit for all services throughout the Great Fifty Days. It is also used throughout the year at baptisms and funerals.

EASTER

"Hail thee Festival Day!" The Queen of all the seasons. Without the glorious event commemorated and celebrated this day – the resurrection of our Lord Jesus Christ from the dead – the rest would not exist. Without Easter there can be no Christmas. The church would not exist, and among peoples we would be the most miserable.

The Great Vigil of Easter which marks the beginning of the Easter season is possibly the most glorious service in the Prayer Book and is gradually beginning to take its rightful place as such, as more and more parishes observe it. In the notes concerning the Vigil (page 284, BCP) and in the rubrics are found specific guidelines for the observance of the ancient ceremonies which, among other things features the lighting of the "new fire."

Fig.8–9
Example of Paschal Candle

Many parishes throughout the country have the congregation bring bells to the Vigil. Following the renewal of baptismal vows in the candlelit Vigil liturgy, the celebrant says, *"Alleluia. Christ is risen."* The people respond: *" The Lord is risen indeed. Alleluia!"* The church lights come on. The organ, the choir, perhaps even a brass choir, and/or other instruments spring to life — and the congregation begin ringing their bells as the glorious procession begins!

Fig. 8–10
Example of Easter Banner

Fig. 8–11
Example of Mesh Wire Cross
Flowered in Children's Procession

The Eucharist, which follows the Great Vigil, is the first Mass of Easter; therefore it, and all other Easter Liturgies of Easter Day, should be the most beautiful and joyful a parish can muster.

White vestments are used, but altar flowers need *not* be all lillies. In fact, perhaps they should be whatever is in bloom. One of the most beautiful floral offerings we ever saw was a three-foot high cross "flowered" by the children of the parish, who brought the flowers from home and put them in a mesh wire cruciform themselves (with the help of Sunday School teachers) during the procession. They brought everything from orchids to dandelions: red and pink roses and carnations, purple iris, yellow daffodils, and even some white lillies. It was a glorious gift of love!

Fig. 8–12
The Ascension

ASCENSION

The Feast of the Ascension (the Thursday forty days after Easter) celebrates Christ's ascension into heaven. It is a major feast and is commemorated only on the day itself.

The Easter Season lasts fifty days and climaxes with the Feast of Pentecost.

PENTECOST

Pentecost, also called *Whitsunday*, commemorates the descent of the Holy Spirit. The mighty acts of redemption – the resurrection, ascension, and the gift of the Spirit – belong together, each being an inseparable part of the other. God the Father created us; God the Son redeems us; God the Holy Spirit sanctifies and enables us.

Fig. 8–13
Symbol of the Holy Spirit

THE SEASON AFTER PENTECOST

All of the rest of the Sundays of the year are called *Sundays after Pentecost.* As the first part of the year dealt with events of our Lord's earthly life, teachings, passion, and resurrection, the second half, after Pentecost, celebrates the continuing work of Christ in his Church through the Holy Spirit, between his first and second Advent, *"until his coming again."*

PRINCIPAL FEASTS

Having dealt rather summarily with the seasons of the church year, let's take a look at the principal feasts observed. They take precedence over any other day, including Sunday. Turn again to page 15 of the BCP, where you will find them listed. They are:

- Easter Day
- Ascension Day
- The Day of Pentecost
- Trinity Sunday
- All Saints' Day (November 1)
- Christmas Day (December 25)
- The Epiphany (January 6)

But, as always, it takes the exception to prove the rule. All Saints' may always be observed on the Sunday following November 1, in *addition* to its observance on the fixed date.

You have just engraved on your minds that all Sundays of the year are feasts of our Lord Jesus Christ and only those already stated take precedence, only to discover that:

- the Holy Name (formerly called the Circumcision), January 1;
- the Presentation of our Lord Jesus Christ in the Temple, February 2; and
- the Transfiguration of Our Lord Jesus Christ, August 6

also take precedence of a Sunday.

There are a couple of other exceptions, too.

- The feast of the dedication of a church, or
- a patronal festival

may be transferred to a Sunday — except during Advent, Lent, and Easter.

For a list of the holy days regularly observed throughout the year check the lists on pages 16 and 17 of the Book of Common Prayer.

DAYS OF FASTING

There are two days of fasting: Ash Wednesday and Good Friday. On these days no solid food and no meat dishes are eaten until after sundown. Those excepted from fasting are children, the elderly, men or women whose work is of such a strenuous physical nature that going without solid food would be a danger to themselves or others, and people who are ill.

Further, there are days observed by special acts of discipline and self-denial:
- Ash Wednesday,
- the forty days of Lent, and
- all other Fridays of the year, except for: those between Christmas and Epiphany; the Great Fifty Days of Easter; and any Feasts of the Lord which happen to be on a Friday.

Why Fridays? To commemorate what our Lord did for us that Friday afternoon on the hill outside Jerusalem.

On pages 19 through 30 of the BCP there is a month-by-month calendar of all the holy days, followed by a list of the *Titles of the Seasons, Sundays and Major Holy Days observed in this Church throughout the Year*.

Now, that wasn't too bad was it? If you get confused occasionally, don't panic or *Mea Culpa* yourself into hysteria. We all forget from time to time. Simply open the Prayer Book, look at the Ordo Calendar, or ask your priest. If your priest doesn't know off hand, you can look it up together.

LITURGICAL COLORS

Somewhere, over – or under – the rainbow, almost any color you can name is being used in churches for vestments, altar hangings, banners, and so forth. It was not until the Tridentine Missal of 1570 that colors were defined by rubric (liturgical instruction) in the Roman Catholic Church and not until the nineteenth century that the system was universally accepted.

Thus shatters the myth that the code for the symbolism of colors is only slightly less inviolate than the Ten Commandments. In the early church the only indications of the use of a particular color was the use of white for baptisms and for funerals. As the use of vestments became more common, white seems to have been the preferred color. This continued until the twelfth century, when various colors began to be used.

Early sacramentaries merely stated that the best vestments were to be used for major feasts regardless of color. (One even cautions the clergy not to blow their noses on the chasubles!)

COLORS USED TODAY

However, the use of colors is fairly consistent in the Episcopal Church, even given the influence of the liturgical movement. The colors most predominantly in use and the symbolism of each are as follows:

White

White is used as a symbol for purity. You will see white used on occasions that commemorate Christ's life on earth, like Christmas, Easter, and Epiphany. The purity of white is appropriate for new birth, and therefore is used for baptism – and is also used for other important events in the lives of people, such as weddings and funerals. As stated in an earlier module, white is the presence of all colors.

Red

Red is used to symbolize both the fire of the Holy Spirit and martyrdom. Since it is also the frequent color of choice for ordinations and consecrations, one is left somewhat confused as to whether the red is symbolic of the descent of the Holy Spirit upon the newly ordained (or the new bishop), or in anticipation of a new church martyr. (Perhaps it all depends on the vestries and the Standing Committees of the world – and sometimes the altar guilds, too!)

Purple

Purple is used for penitence and to indicate sorrow. However, purple is also used as a symbol for royalty (as in "royal purple").

Green

Green is the symbol for life (otherwise why would the walls of most hospitals be painted green). It is also the symbol for growth, fertility, and spring. If you doubt the appropriateness of this symbolism, examine the green mold you discover the next time you clean out the refrigerator during spring cleaning.

Blue

Blue is also used as a symbol for penitence. No one is quite certain whether blue or purple provide a more meaningful outward sign of a contrite spirit. However, blue is also used for penitential preparation, as during Advent. It is also traditionally the color assigned to the Blessed Virgin Mary.

Rose

The color rose is used for the Fourth Sunday in Lent and Third Sunday in Advent. Most people refer to it as "pink," but we more sophisticated folk know *a rose by any other name is still. . .*

WHEN TO USE WHAT

Advent

Many churches use purple, yet many use blue to mark the difference between this season and Lent. Check with your priest to determine preference or parish tradition.

Christmas

White is used, as stated earlier, because it is an occasion that commemorates the beginning of our Lord's life on earth.

Epiphany

Use white for the Feast of the Epiphany, but change to green for the season.

Ash Wednesday

Many churches use purple; however many others use what is called a "Lenten array" – natural-colored linen bordered with purple and red or black and red.

Passion Sunday

(Palm Sunday) and Holy Week: use dark red or Lenten array, or purple.

Maundy Thursday

Most churches use red or Lenten array. Some parishes still use white.

Good Friday

Dark red; Lenten array; purple. (Not all at the same time. Select one of the three.)

Easter

White or gold for Easter. White for the season.

Pentecost

Red, as a symbol of the Holy Spirit.

Trinity Sunday

White.

After Pentecost

All Sundays after Pentecost until Advent use green. (So make sure its a restful green. You'll see a lot of it.)

All Saints' Day

(and the Sunday following) White or gold.

COLORS USED FOR MAJOR FEASTS AND HOLY DAYS

OCCASION	WHITE	RED	PURPLE	GREEN	BLUE	ROSE	LENTEN ARRAY	DARK RED	GOLD
Advent			optional		optional	3rd Sunday			
Christmas	always								
Epiphany Day	always								
Epiphany Season				always					
Ash Wednesday			optional				optional		
Lent						4th Sunday	optional		
Palm Sunday			optional				optional	optional	
Maundy Thursday	optional						preferred		
Good Friday			optional				optional	optional	
Easter Day	optional								optional
Easter Season	always								
Pentecost		always							
Trinity Sunday	always								
Sundays after Pentecost				always					
All Saints Day	optional								optional

COLORS FOR OTHER TIMES:

OCCASION	WHITE	RED	GREEN	BLUE
Feasts of our Lord	always			
Apostles, martyrs or evangelists		always		
St. John the Evangelist	always			
Confession of Peter	always			
Confession of Paul	always			
Holy Cross Day		always		
St. Michael and All Angels	always			
Rogation Days	optional		optional	
Feasts of St. Mary	optional			optional
Thanksgiving Day	always			
Independence Day	always			

KEY TO CHARTS:

COLOR ALWAYS USED ▦

COLOR PREFERRED ▨

OPTIONAL COLOR ▥

COLORS FOR OTHER TIMES

Feasts of our Lord	(i.e., Presentation, Transfiguration) White
Apostles, martyrs or evangelists	Red
St. John the Evangelist	White
Confession of Peter	White
Conversion of Paul	White
Holy Cross Day	Red
St. Michael and All Angels	White
Rogation Days	White or purple
In Commemoration of St. Mary	(Annunciation, Visitation, St. Mary the Virgin) Blue or white.
Thanksgiving Day	White
Independence Day	White
Commemoration of black letter days in the calendar	(martyrs) (except when red is used) White.

There is a color for the various occasions for which the Book of Common Prayer has collects as well.

While these are the colors typically used, some churches adapt them for particular buildings and types of architecture. One sees bright colors used on joyous occasions: yellows, bright blues, even oranges and pinks; or tans, browns, dark red, or dark blue used on occasions of penitence and sorrow.

More and more there is a tendency to use somber colors for vestments on somber occasions and light, bright ones in festal seasons. Just be sure they are beautiful and remember that beautiful doesn't necessarily mean expensive.

SUMMARY

The Calendar of the Church Year is found on page 15 of the Book of Common Prayer. No one is expected to remember when the church celebrates various saints' feasts. These are easily found on Ordo Calendars.

The basic framework upon which the church year is structured is the seven-day week with Sunday counted as the first day. The church year divides roughly into two periods: one representing Christ in his earthly life; the other representing his reign through the Spirit in his church until his coming again.

The Church seasons are: Advent, Christmas, Epiphany, Lent, Easter, and the season after Pentecost. The BCP gives precedence to the celebration of Sundays over saints' days. Each Sunday is a "little Easter." (Does this mean you can justify a new "little Easter" outfit for the other fifty-one Sundays each year? – But, it's fun to think about. Just imagine! Fifty-one more "little Easter" parades down Fifth Avenue in New York!)

According to the BCP (page 15), the church year consists of two cycles of feasts and holy days: one dependent upon Easter Day; the other, upon December 25, Christmas Day.

It's important to know the date for Easter because so much of the Church calendar depends on it. On page 882 of the BCP, *A Table to Find Easter Day* makes it fast, fun and easy to calculate Easter for any year from 1900 through 2089. (That should cover the life of this training manual.)

Once you know the date of Easter, the *Table to Find Movable Feasts and Holy Days* provides a quick reference for the major feasts and holy days.

The church year begins with the First Sunday of Advent, always four Sundays before Christmas Day, and ends with Midnight Mass on Christmas Eve. Advent is not a "little Lent." The whole atmosphere of Advent should be quiet, in joyful expectation and preparatory anticipation, mixed with penitence.

The Christmas season begins with the first Mass on Christmas Eve and continues through the twelve days of Christmas until the Feast of the Epiphany. The feasts of Christmas and Epiphany developed as a means to Christianize pagan festivals related to the winter solstice.

Epiphany comes on the twelfth day of Christmas, January 6. It commemorates the manifestation of Christ to the Gentiles. It is the day we celebrate the wise men coming to worship the Christ Child.

The First Sunday after the Epiphany is celebrated as the Feast of the Baptism of Our Lord. The last day of Epiphany is Shrove Tuesday. Ash Wednesday marks the beginning of the Lenten season. Ashes used on this day are obtained by burning palms from the previous Palm Sunday. The season of Lent is the forty days before Easter, not counting the Sundays.

Holy Week begins on Palm Sunday, and extends to the Eucharist concluding the Easter Vigil. Holy Week is the liturgical reenactment of the events in the last week of the earthly life of our Lord. On Maundy Thursday we remember the Lord's Last Supper with the apostles – and the institution of the Eucharist. Good Friday is the most solemn of all days in the Christian calendar. It is a day of deepest mourning, marked with special services and observances. No Eucharist is celebrated on Holy Saturday.

The Great Vigil of Easter marks the beginning of the fifty-day Easter season.

Pentecost, also called Whitsunday, commemorates the descent of the Holy Spirit. The remaining Sundays of the year are called Sundays after Pentecost.

The principal feasts observed by the church are listed on page 15 of the BCP, and holy days are listed on pages 16 and 17. We have two "official" days of fasting – Ash Wednesday and Good Friday. But there are other days observed by special acts of discipline and self-denial.

On pages 19 through 30 of the BCP there is a month-by-month calendar of all the holy days followed by a list of the *Titles of the Seasons, Sundays and Major Holy Days observed in this Church throughout the Year*.

Almost all colors are being used in churches for vestments, altar hangings, and banners. The use of colors is fairly consistent in today's Episcopal Church. **White** is symbolic of purity, and is used on occasions that commemorate Christ's life on earth, and for Baptisms, weddings and funerals. **Red** is used to symbolize the fire of the Holy Spirit and martyrdom. **Purple** symbolizes penitence and is used to indicate sorrow. It is also a symbol for royalty. **Green** is the symbol for life, growth, fertility, and spring. **Blue** also is used as a symbol for penitence; for example, it is used for penitential preparation, as during Advent. Blue is also traditionally the color assigned to the Blessed Virgin Mary. **Rose** is used for the Fourth Sunday in Lent and Third Sunday in Advent.

If you feel comfortable with the information contained in Module 8, proceed to the progress check. If not, you may wish to review the module again before completing the progress check.

WHITE
IS THE
PRESENCE
OF
ALL
COLOR

MODULE 8
PROGRESS CHECK

Respond to the questions by filling in the blanks. Feel free to use the text of the module to assist you in answering.

1. The _____ _____ is our best way to keep track of when the church celebrates various saints' feasts.

2. _____ _____ is the most solemn of all days in the Christian Calendar.

3. *A Table to Find Easter Day* is found on page _____ of the BCP.

4. The basic framework upon which the church year is structured is the _____ with _____ counted as the first day.

5. The appropriate color for the following:
   - Advent   _____.

   - Ash Wednesday   _____.

   - Palm Sunday   _____.

   - Maundy Thursday   _____.

   - Good Friday   _____.

(ANSWERS ON THE BACK OF THIS PAGE)

**MODULE 8
ANSWER SHEET**

Respond to the questions by filling in the blanks. Feel free to use the text of the module to assist you in answering.

1. The **Ordo Calendar** is our best way to keep track of when the church celebrates various saints' feasts.

2. **Good Friday** is the most solemn of all days in the Christian calendar.

3. *A Table to Find Easter Day* is found on page **882** of the BCP.

4. The basic framework upon which the church year is structured is the **seven-day cycle** with **Sunday** counted as the first day.

5. The appropriate color for the following:
    *   Advent   **Purple or Blue.**

    *   Ash Wednesday   **Purple or Lenten Array.**

    *   Palm Sunday   **Dark Red or Lenten Array.**

    *   Maundy Thursday **Red, Lenten Array or White**

    *   Good Friday   **Dark Red, Lenten Array or Purple.**

Now, look over your answers. If you feel comfortable that you understand the material in Module 8, please continue to Module 9. If not, you may wish to review the material again.

MODULE 9
THE SERVICES OF THE CHURCH

*Now that we know what play is showing and when it is showing
we need to understand how to set up the stage for each performance.*

TIME:
Approximately 2 hours.

OBJECTIVE:
Given the contents of Module 9, you will be able to demonstrate an understanding of the various worship services of the Episcopal Church by responding to simple fill-in-the-blank questions with 100% accuracy.

ACTIVITIES:
- Read the text of the module
- Complete Progress Check
- Complete Module Exercises

MATERIAL REQUIRED:
- This Module
- Pen or Pencil
- Progress Check

OTHER RESOURCE MATERIAL:
- 1979 Book of Common Prayer
- The Book of Occasional Services

COURSE MAP

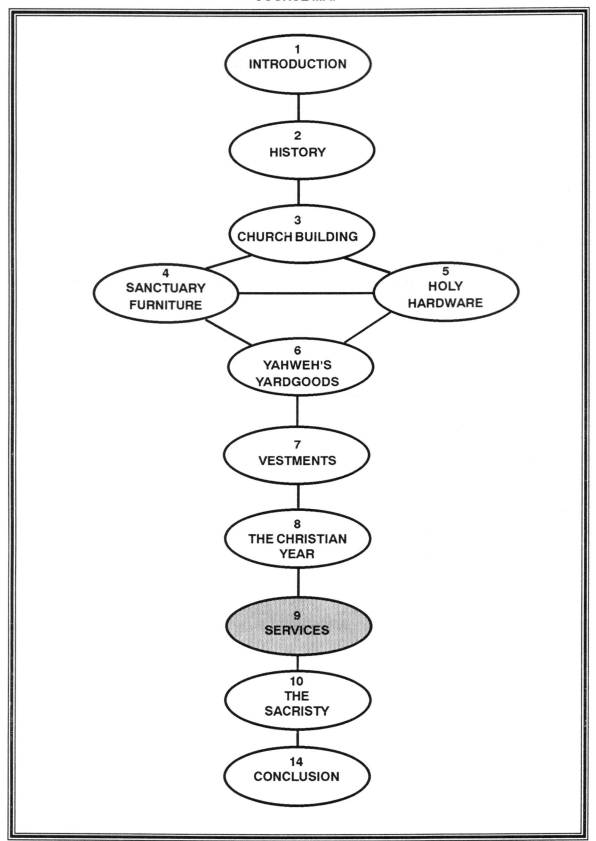

MODULE 9
THE SERVICES OF THE CHURCH

INTRODUCTION

Everything we have discussed thus far in our course has pointed us to this module. In previous modules we have talked about things: buildings, furniture, vessels, vestments, linens, and even colors. In Module 9 all of these "things" are combined and we see how they are used in concert to provide the appropriate settings for the various services of the church.

Dominical Sacraments

The Episcopal Church teaches and provides for seven sacraments. The first two, common to all Christians, and essential for membership and continuing life in the Body of Christ (the church), are Holy Baptism and Holy Communion. They are sometimes called the *Dominical Sacraments,* those specifically instituted and commanded by our Lord (*Domine* in Latin). *"Go ye therefore into the world baptising in the name of the Father, Son, and Holy Spirit."* And, at the Last Supper: *"Do this. . . in remembrance of me."*

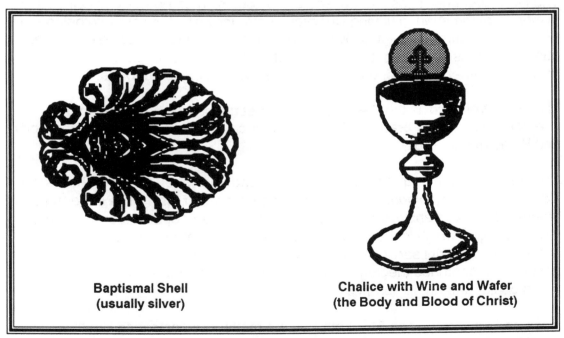

Baptismal Shell **(usually silver)**	**Chalice with Wine and Wafer** **(the Body and Blood of Christ)**

Fig. 9-1
Symbols of Baptism and Holy Communion

Minor Sacraments

The five lesser or minor sacraments are available to all, but not essential in the same sense as the first two. They are Holy Confirmation, Holy Matrimony, Holy Orders, Penance, and Holy Unction.

Obviously not everyone enters Holy Orders, nor does everyone get married. But it is also obvious after a cursory glance at the Prayer Book and Book of Occasional Services that the services of the church are there to mark our physical and spiritual lives almost as rites of passage from the cradle to the grave. *"Lo, I am with you always, even to the end of the world."*

To look at the Dominical Sacraments in chronological order (according to our lives), we should discuss Baptism first. However, from the viewpoint of the altar guild, the Eucharist (or Mass) requires more effort, so we will begin with a discussion of the Holy Eucharist.

THE HOLY EUCHARIST

The Holy Eucharist is the principal act of worship on the Lord's Day and other major feasts. This fact is obvious and inescapable when one studies the Prayer Book. The Eucharist is the climax of the sacrament of Holy Baptism, all the pastoral services, and occasional services. At ordinations to the priesthood it symbolizes the entrance of the newly ordained into the full priesthood of Christ.

The Holy Eucharist is the symbol and efficacious sign of the Body of Christ. It is *symbolic* of the sharing, loving Christian community which it calls into being – or *effects* – and empowers. It is also sacrament and sacrifice. A *sacrament* is an outward and visible sign of the inward and invisible Presence of Christ. It is *sacrifice* in what our Lord, out of love for us, was willing to do for us.

The *Real Presence* is the theological term that the church has given to the everyday elements of bread and wine, that, once consecrated, become the Body and Blood of our Lord.

Our Lord, that night with his apostles, took bread and wine. He said *"This is my Body. . . This is my blood. . . Do this in remembrance of me."* The word "remembrance" is a poor translation, in English, of the full intent of the Hebrew words, the meaning of which is more nearly *"for the recalling of me to your midst."* It is not quite a memorial service. It does no good to question the manner or mode of the gift. For centuries theologians have written weighty tomes on the subject which could, and do, fill libraries.

Lines attributed to Queen Elizabeth I on the matter run something like this:
> ***"His were the hands that break it;***
> ***His were the lips that spake it;***
> ***What His Word doth make it;***
> ***That I believe and take it."***

The futility of trying to explain the doctrine of the Real Presence was forever laid to rest for one parish priest by a child in First Communion Class. Finishing-up the course, the good father had taken the class into the sacristy for a "hands-on" session so that they could see and touch vessels and vestments. He took uncon- secrated wafers passing them out as each child held them in inquisitive fingers.

"This is bread," he said in serious tones.

"Funny looking bread," came a child's simple statement.

The priest agreed and asked, "What does it become when it is blessed?"

They demonstrated that they'd done their homework with a chorus of, "The Body of Christ." Then the priest got them all to agree that after it became the Body of Christ it was not to be played-with. It was to be eaten.

Taking a chalice, the priest handed it to a child who looked at it very carefully and then also very carefully handed it to the next child. When it got back around the circle, the priest held up water and wine. "What are these?"

"Water and wine," his charges chorused.

"What do they become when they are blessed?"

"The Blood of Jesus," they sang out.

To this day he doesn't know why he said, "This is bread and it becomes the Body of Jesus. This is water and wine; it becomes the Blood of Jesus. How in the world do you suppose that happens?"

No chorus this time. The priest had gone beyond their lesson. Just then a little voice said loudly and clearly, "I don't know. God does it."

God does, indeed, do it! That's all we can ever know. It's enough! Our theology is further borne out in the way we are communicated: the Body broken and given to us. The one cup shared by the family around his table.

But it is also evident in the reverent way any of the Sacrament is disposed of following communion. The Prayer Book (pp. 408-409) says: "If any. . . remain, apart from any which may be required for the Communion of the sick, or of oth- ers. . . or for the administration of Communion by a deacon, . . . the celebrant or deacon, and other communicants, reverently eat and drink it, either after the Communion of the people or after the Dismissal."

In the sacristy the theology is again asserted in that chalices, paten, and ciborium are rinsed and the water poured into a special sink (or *piscina*) which carries it directly to the earth. Corporals are shaken into the piscina; purificators are rinsed and the water also disposed down the piscina. (In the absence of a piscina pouring these directly on the ground outside the sacristy is acceptable.)

If an altar guild member has any doubts as to whether or not elements have been consecrated, a safe rule is: 1) If it's on the altar after Mass, it has been. 2) If it is on the credence table, it hasn't. Unconsecrated wine may be poured back into the bottle from the flagon or cruet. Unconsecrated wafers are put away for future use.

If a wafer is found in the nave or narthex after a service, assume that it is consecrated. It should either be consumed or taken to the sacristy and put down the piscina.

ALTAR GUILD DUTIES

Now that we have looked at the theology of Holy Communion, Eucharist, the Mass (or whatever you prefer to call it), let's look at how this impacts on the altar guild. If we assume that the Eucharist is the principal service of the church, there are things that must be done on a regularly scheduled basis to prepare for the service – or services, in most cases.

As a rule, altar guild teams are assigned to weekly general cleaning duties, usually done on Saturdays to prepare for Sunday's services. Each parish altar guild has unique needs, but the following is a sample of the types of tasks that must be accomplished weekly:
- Clean the sanctuary, including dusting all furniture, sweeping/vacuuming the floor of the sanctuary, and removing candlewax droppings.
- Change the fair linen, frontal, etc., if necessary.
- Polish all brass and silver articles, if needed.
- Clean and set up eucharistic vessels for the first Mass scheduled for Sunday (using appropriately colored burse and veil).
- Set out vestments on the priest's vesting table, according to the color of the day.
- Set up Altar Books, Gospel and Epistle Books.
- Check/replenish all candles including sanctuary and votive candles, wicks, followers, and lighters.
- Clean sacristy, including all counter tops, sinks, piscina. Sweep/vacuum if appropriate.

EXERCISE 9–1
CREATE A CHECK-OFF LIST OF
WEEKLY ALTAR GUILD TASKS AT _YOUR_ PARISH

Since every parish has different supplies, equipment, schedules, etc., it is important for you to know what weekly cleaning and set-up responsibilities must be done by your altar guild. The check-off list on the next page is taken from a particular parish; however, it can serve as a guide for you to create your own check-off list. There may be a similar list posted in the sacristy at your church. If so, checking your list will be very easy. If not, discuss your check-off sheet with your altar guild director or your rector.

Now, use this sheet to create your own Check-Off List of Weekly Duties. (You may need extra paper. If so, you may want to make extra copies of this page of the manual.)

WEEKLY ALTAR GUILD CHECK-OFF LIST

FLOWERS	Initial when complete	Comments
1. Arrange flowers		
CLEANING .		
2. Polish Brass:		
• Torches		
• Lighters		
• Tops of Office Lights		
3. Thoroughly wash, dry, and buff silver		
4. Clean cruets.		
5. Clean piscina.		
6. Clean:		
counter tops		
sink		
window ledges		
7. Vacuum:		
confessional		
acolyte sacristy		
altar guild working sacristy		
priests' sacristy		
8. Dust all areas in priests' sacristy		
9. Clean and refill Holy Water Bowls.		
10. Clean thurible and incense area.		
11. Sweep floor in sanctuary		
12. Dust all furniture in sacristy		
13. Arrange books/hymnals on sedilia		
CANDLES		
14. Replace candles in torches as needed.		
15. Check pavement candles.		
16. Check wicks in lighters.		
17. Check/replace votives in nave.		
ALTAR		
18. Change frontal (if required)		
19. Change fair linen (if required)		
20. Check sanctuary lamp		
21. Set out clean vesting cloths (if needed)		
22. Set out vestments for Mass		
23. Set out eucharistic vessels		
24. Mark Mass books		
GENERAL		
25. Check supplies and leave list of needs on bulletin board.		

Fig. 9–2
Example of Weekly Check-Off List

EXERCISE 9–2
CREATE A CHECK-OFF LIST FOR
MASS SET-UP

Now that you have the routine down, use this sheet to create your own check-off list of what you have to do to set up for all Eucharists (not specific ones) at your parish. (We will cover specific Masses later.) An example of the types of duties that might be included on your list is found in Figure 9–3. (If you need extra paper, make copies of this page of the manual.)

Check your list against that of your altar guild or discuss it with your rector.

SET-UP CHECK-OFF LIST FOR ALL EUCHARISTS

SET-UP CHECK-OFF LIST FOR ALL EUCHARISTS

1. Vested chalice and back-up chalice, if one is necessary, to be placed on the credence table in the sanctuary at all Masses.

2. Cruets, lavabo bowl and towel, bread box are placed on the credence table in the sanctuary. (For Sunday Masses the cruets and ciborium are placed on the credence table at the back of the church.)

3. Place the two Eucharistic candles on the altar for all Masses, a hand's-width from the sides and back of the altar. Six office lights on gradine at all Masses. They are not lit at Low Masses.

4. Place waxed corporal on altar. Open a corporal and place on Altar on top of waxed corporal. (Check with your rector for desired corporal set-up.)

5. Place the Gospel Book on the Altar. (Gold book on Sundays and Major Feasts, red and gold leather book for Low Masses.)

6. Altar Book with blue dot on inside cover at Low Masses. Sunday at 10:00 a.m. Mass place the Altar Book on the credence shelf on the gospel side of the sanctuary.

7. Place the lesson book – Lectionary – on the lectern. (The epistle side of the sanctuary.)

8. The small red leather Book of Common Prayer and the intercession book (red with gold cross) are placed on the prie-dieu at the sedelia (priest's bench) at all Masses. Altar Book without blue dot is also placed on the prie-dieu.

Fig. 9–3
Example of Set-Up Check-Off List For All Eucharists

LOW, MEDIUM, AND HIGH

Now that you have created a check-off list of things to be done every week, and another for setting up for <u>every</u> Eucharist, let's think about the different types of masses for which the altar guild must prepare.

Whether your parish is considered "high church," Anglo-Catholic, "low church," or somewhere in between, there are basically three types of eucharistic services that are conducted in most Episcopal Churches in the U.S. (whether weekly, monthly, or whenever the mood strikes):

- **Low Masses**
  A Low Mass is frequently celebrated as the early service on Sundays and the regularly scheduled weekday Masses. The term "Low Mass" usually refers to a Eucharist without music and with a minimal number (or no) servers. The only person required in the sanctuary for a Low Mass is the celebrant. Many times, but not always, there is no homily (sermon) given at a Low Mass.

- **Family Masses**
  We are calling this "Family Mass" to cover a "medium" level mass (either Rite I or Rite II), with music and a sermon. For churches that have three "levels" of masses each Sunday, this is usually the service that is either before, after, or during Sunday School – and the one in which the children from Sunday School participate in some form.

- **Solemn High Masses**
  In spite of what a lot of people believe, a Solemn High Mass can be done using either Rite I or Rite II. It usually implies that there is incense, sanctus bells and that the lessons are sung. The music can be anything from Gregorian Chant to guitars and drums. The celebrant may celebrate facing the congregation or the east wall.

The point of all this is simply that, as a member of the altar guild, you need to know the "level" of the Eucharistic services conducted on a regular basis at your parish.

On the next few pages there are exercises similar to the ones that you have just completed that will help you determine the responsibilities expected of you before and after Low, Family, and Solemn High Masses. If any of the exercises do not apply to your parish, simply skip them.

EXERCISE 9–3
CREATE A CHECK-OFF LIST FOR
THINGS THAT MUST BE DONE BEFORE LOW MASS

Figure 9–4 contains examples of details that you may need to consider. Check your list against that of your Altar Guild or discuss it with your rector.

BEFORE LOW MASS

BEFORE LOW MASS

1. Turn on sanctuary and nave lights.

2. Unlock front door of church.

3. Check tabernacle and remove dust cover from altar.

4. Place office lights in position – which may or may not be lighted.

5. Place flowers in position in the sanctuary. Leave room for the Priest and server to move around the altar.

6. Put credence cloths on all credence tables.

7. Place Eucharistic candles on the Altar.

8. Place alms basins on credence table at the back of the church.

9. Set out all vessels and books, when no server or M.C. is present.

10. Set out votive lamps at any shrines and check for sufficient votive candles.

11. Set out pavement candles and kneeler-cushions in the sanctuary and kneeler-cushions at altar rail.

12. Please leave sacristy before the priest and servers begin to vest.

Fig. 9–4
Example of "Before" Low Mass Check-Off List

EXERCISE 9–4
CREATE A CHECK-OFF LIST FOR
THINGS THAT MUST BE DONE AFTER LOW MASS

Figure 9–5 contains examples of details that you may need to consider. Check your list against that of your altar guild or discuss it with your rector.

AFTER LOW MASS

AFTER LOW MASS

1. Remove eucharistic candles from altar if they are not to be used for a later service.

2. Remove eucharistic vessels from credence table. Unvest chalice and clean chalice with boiling water over the piscina. Rinse crumbs from paten into piscina. Pour water from lavabo bowl into piscina. Rinse purificator over the piscina with hot water also.

3. Wash chalice, paten, lavabo bowl, cruets, and ciborium in hot soapy water. (DO NOT IMMERSE bases of vessels – rinse and dry thoroughly.) Refill cruets to designated amounts.

4. Revest chalice and set up for the next scheduled Mass.

5. Refill ciborium with required number of wafers.

6. Reset vestments for next scheduled Mass.

7. Remove alms basins and any money from votive and alms box. (On Sundays, return alms basins for next service.)

8. Take home soiled linens to clean. (Each team decides how they will rotate linen duty.)

Fig. 9–5
Example of "After" Low Mass Check-Off List

EXERCISE 9–5
CREATE A CHECK-OFF LIST FOR
THINGS THAT MUST BE DONE BEFORE FAMILY MASS

Figure 9–6 contains examples of details that you may need to consider. Time (or lack of it) between the end of an early Low Mass (e.g., on Sundays) and the beginning of a Family Mass may be a factor. Therefore, the "before" tasks for the Family Mass would have to include the same activities as the "after" responsibilities of Low Mass. Check your list against that of your altar guild or discuss it with your rector.

BEFORE FAMILY MASS

BEFORE FAMILY MASS

1. Half-fill large cruets and revest chalice. Refill ciborium with required number of wafers. Have server(s) or subdeacon set out holy vessels for the Family Mass.

   Sanctuary Credence Table:
   - Vested Chalice and Burse
   - Unvested Chalice
   - Small Pewter Ewer with designated amount of extra wine.

   Credence Table at Back of Nave:
   - Cruets (with handles turned so that ushers carry by handles)
   - Ciborium
   - Alms Basins (with bulletins)

   Sanctuary Credence Shelf (epistle side)
   - Altar Book

   Sanctuary Credence Shelf (gospel side)
   - Cruet Stopper Dish
   - Lavabo and Lavabo Towel

2. Reset vestments for Family Mass. May need extra stole(s).

3. Leave sacristy before altar party arrives to vest.

Fig. 9–6
Example of "Before" Family Mass Check-Off List

EXERCISE 9–6
CREATE A CHECK-OFF LIST FOR
THINGS THAT MUST BE DONE AFTER FAMILY MASS

Figure 9–7 contains examples of details that you may need to consider. The "after" tasks for the Family Mass will depend on whether or not it is the last Mass of the day. Check your list against that of your altar guild or discuss it with your rector.

AFTER FAMILY MASS

AFTER FAMILY MASS

1. Remove eucharistic vessels from credence table. Unvest chalice and clean chalice with boiling water over the piscina. Rinse crumbs from paten into piscina. Pour water from lavabo bowl into piscina. Rinse purificator over the piscina with hot water also.

2. Wash chalice, paten, lavabo bowl, cruets and ciborium in hot soapy water. (DO NOT IMMERSE bases of vessels – rinse and dry thoroughly.

3. Remove alms basins and place in designated place.

4. If this is the final service of the day:

   • Depending on instructions, reset vessels for next scheduled service, or place vessels in appropriate cabinets, drawers, etc.
   • Either reset vestments or put them away in vestment closet, depending on instructions.
   • Remove flowers from sanctuary, remove altar candles, and credence table covers.
   • Place dust cover over fair linen on altar.

5. Take soiled linen to be cleaned.

Fig. 9–7
Example of "After" Family Mass Check-Off List

EXERCISE 9–7
CREATE A CHECK-OFF LIST FOR
THINGS THAT MUST BE DONE BEFORE SOLEMN HIGH MASS

Figure 9–8 contains examples of details that you may need to consider. Check your list against that of your altar guild or discuss it with your rector.

BEFORE SOLEMN HIGH MASS

BEFORE SOLEMN HIGH MASS

1. Arrive a least 30 minutes before service.

2. Fill large cruets to appropriate amounts and check chalice set-up. Refill ciborium with required number of wafers. Set out holy vessels. (Cruets and ciborium on credence table at back of nave.) Check extra chalice(s) set-up.

3. Check that vestments are set out (including dalmatic,tunicle and cope). May need extra stole(s).

4. Set out gospel book, altar book, etc.

5. Check that thurible, incense, and sanctus bell are set.

6. Check that alms basins are in place.

7. Leave sacristy before altar party vest.

Fig. 9–8
Example of "Before" Solemn High Mass Check-Off List

EXERCISE 9–8
CREATE A CHECK-OFF LIST FOR
THINGS THAT MUST BE DONE AFTER SOLEMN HIGH MASS

Figure 9–9 contains examples of details that you may need to consider. Check your list against that of your altar guild or discuss it with your rector.

AFTER SOLEMN HIGH MASS

AFTER SOLEMN HIGH MASS

1. Remove credence cloths from all credence tables.

2. Turn out lights in nave and sanctuary.

3. Remove appropriate extra candles in nave, side altars, shrines, etc.

4. Remove from Sanctuary:
   a. Everything on the credence table and shelves.
   b. Gospel and Epistle Books, Altar Book and stand.
   c. Flowers and stands.
   d. Everything NOT used at weekly Low Masses.

5. Replace dust cover on Altar.

6. Clean vessels and set up for next scheduled Mass.

7. Lock all silver vessels in cupboard and put alms basins away.

8. Put away vestments on hangers and in appropriately marked drawers.

9. Take soiled linens home to launder.

10. Remove money from votive and alms boxes (if appropriate) in nave and place in assigned place.

Fig. 9–9
Example of "After" Solemn High Mass Check-Off List

HOLY BAPTISM

Baptism is the most important event in the life of a Christian. Its roots are in those rites of initiation common to all cultures: in the Jewish ritual cleansings and washings of the Quamran; in the baptism of repentance of John the Baptist; and in our Lord's command to go into the world and baptize. The anointing and pouring of water upon one's forehead in the name of the Holy Trinity is a sacrament-sign of the inward and indwelling presence of Christ and can never be removed. "You are marked as Christ's own forever." The anointing signifies incorporation into Christ, the Anointed One of God, and into his royal priesthood.

In the early church, adult baptisms were usually a part of the Easter Vigil. Infant baptism quickly became a widespread custom soon after the establishment of Christianity. Pentecost (signifying baptism as receiving the Holy Spirit) and Epiphany (symbolizing baptism as new birth) joined Easter as important days for baptism.

The 1979 BCP stresses the public, corporate, family nature of baptism and restores it to its prominence as the primary sacrament. It states that insofar as possible, baptism is to be reserved for Easter, Pentecost, the Feast of the Baptism of our Lord, All Saints' Day or the Sunday following, and the bishop's visitation. Otherwise the rites are to be administered at a principal Eucharist on a Sunday or other feast.

"Private" baptisms scheduled at other times and not including a Eucharist are not provided for, except in the case of dire emergency, when any Christian may baptize anywhere at any time.

Out of infant baptism came a second rite known as confirmation, when the beliefs of the person who was baptized as an infant are "confirmed," and he or she is given a second anointing with chrism (holy oil) by the bishop.

Altar Guild Duties

There are a few additional responsibilities that fall on the altar guild when baptisms are scheduled. Since we have just about exhausted your patience with "Exercises" in this module, we will simply provide a list of typical additional duties in the form of Figure 9–10. However, be sure to check this list with your altar guild director or rector.

NOTE: 1
ALWAYS CHECK THE CALENDAR FOR FUTURE BAPTISMS.

TYPICAL ALTAR GUILD DUTIES AT BAPTISMS

1. Have ready in the priest's sacristy:
    a. Priest's stole. Use white.
    b. Priest's cope. Use white.

2. Have readily available to be placed on the credence table, next to the font (at the appropriate time), the following:
    a. Large silver pitcher with lukewarm water.
    b. Silver shell and large baptismal towel.
    c. Stock with holy oil.
    d. Baptismal candle with cellophane removed but replaced in the box.
    e. Matches.
    f. Plug for font. Wrap in small piece of Saran Wrap and make secure in font.

3. See that several Prayer Books are available near the font, opened to "Holy Baptism" (page 299).

4. Set paschal candle in place with cross facing baptismal party. Light before service.

5. An altar guild member should sit at the rear of the church during the baptism.

Fig. 9–10
Example of Altar Guild Duties at Baptisms

PASTORAL OFFICES

There are a number of pastoral offices and episcopal services in the Book of Common Prayer for which the altar guild has responsibilities as well. Not to mention the umpteen found in the Book of Occasional Services. They are just that – occasional – for the most part, and can be prepared for in consultation with the clergy.

The pastoral offices which include the other five sacraments, are designed and intended to be celebrated in conjunction with the Holy Eucharist.

CONFIRMATION (pp. 412 - 419)

When this service is performed separately from Holy Baptism, perhaps when the bishop is making a parish visitation and there are no baptisms, a Eucharist with the bishop as celebrant follows. The color is red for confirmations; white if there are also baptisms.

Altar Guild Duties

A list of typical additional duties are found in Figure 9–11. However, be sure to check this list with your altar guild director or rector.

TYPICAL ALTAR GUILD DUTIES FOR CONFIRMATION

1. Prepare as for Solemn High Mass.

2. If your parish uses confirmation veils, check with the rector for the number of confirmands needing veils. Assign someone to be responsible for putting veils on persons to be confirmed (can be one of the mothers).

3. Reserve first three pews for confirmands and sponsors.

4. Arrange appropriate flowers if no memorial.

5. Place bishop's chair in sanctuary.

6. Set out bishop's vestments on rack by priest's sacristy mirror. mitre, stole, and crozier to the left on vesting table. M.C. is responsible for holy oil and general set-up.

Fig. 9–11
Example of Altar Guild Duties at Confirmations

MARRIAGE (The Celebration and Blessing of a Marriage)

Worthy of note in passing, perhaps, is that the New Testament contains no information about a Christian marriage ritual. It would appear historically from other sources that marriages often took place on Sunday, the Holy Eucharist following the exchange of vows.

In the 1549 Prayer Book, Cranmer wrote the service largely from medieval rites and German Reformation church orders. In this rite the marriage took place in the church after Morning Prayer and Litany and before the Eucharist.

Our Prayer Book of 1979 again sets the rite in context of the Liturgy of the Word and Sacrament. But it also provides for "The Blessing of a Civil Marriage" (pp. 433-434) and "An Order for Marriage" (pp. 435-436). The Book of Occasional Services has a rite for the "Anniversary of a Marriage" (pp. 144-146 in 1st edition; pp. 159-161 in 2nd edition).

Altar Guild Duties

Perhaps no other sacrament of the Church has a wider variety of impact on altar guilds than weddings. Some churches have a separate "wedding co-ordinator" who may or may not be a part of the altar guild. Others divide the work among the teams that are normally on duty for the week. Be sure to check with your altar guild director and rector for the procedures that are appropriate for your parish.

The following figure provides some samples of the types of activities required from the altar guild (or wedding co-ordinator). We have also included a sample of a pre-wedding form that should be filled out in discussions with the bride and groom (and the bride's mother!).

TYPICAL ALTAR GUILD DUTIES FOR WEDDINGS

Rehearsal:
The priest takes care of the rehearsal alone. If there is a visiting priest, altar guild members should be present at the rehearsal to unlock the sacristy, take care of the lighting, show the priest the vestments available, etc.

Flowers:
Flowers used at the altar (on the predella) must be left as a thank offering. Other flower arrangements may be placed in the sanctuary or in the narthex and may be removed following the ceremony. You may have to wage war with the florist to assure room is left for the altar party to move around within the sanctuary. (They usually become more docile when you inform them that if flowers are not placed correctly, the service will not take place!)

If flowers are for the altar, they should be arranged in the church's containers, which may be taken to the florist.

Candles:
For Nuptial Mass, light two eucharistic candles on the altar. The six candles on the gradine are lit at all weddings. Altar guild or acolytes light candles before the guests arrive. Additional candles and/or candelabra brought by florist may result in the same confrontation as with flowers – and with the same result.

Vestments: White with red: surplice, stole, cincture, and cope.

Nuptial Mass: White eucharistic vestments. (The priest may celebrate in cope and stole.)

Kneeler: Place kneeler in center of sanctuary.

Assembling the Bridal Party:
The party assembles in the parish hall. They proceed to the church and arrive in the narthex two or three minutes before the ceremony is due to start. The groom, best man, and groomsmen will enter from the sacristy. The ushers will already be in the narthex.

During the Ceremony:
Close outside doors to lessen noise from the street. Receive late guests, accept telegrams, etc.

Photography:
Absolutely no pictures may be taken during the ceremony. Pictures may be taken as the couple start the retiring procession at the end of the ceremony. If the priest is needed for photographs after the ceremony, please let him or her know before vestments are removed.

After the Ceremony:
Clear away all things brought out for the ceremony, and put them in their appropriate places. Close the front door. Turn off all fans and lights. Reset for next service.

Fig. 9–12
Example of Altar Guild Duties at Weddings

ALTAR GUILD WEDDING INFORMATION FORM

Bride's Name _____   Groom's Name _____

Address _____   Address _____

_____   _____

Phone _____   Phone_____

Date of Wedding _____   Time _____

Priest Officiating _____   Nuptial Mass? _____

_____

Conference with Altar Guild Member: Date _____   Time _____

Number of Guests _____   (Church accommodates _____.)

Available parking spaces: _____. No parking signs placed in parking lot on wedding day.

Reception in Parish Hall? _____

Bows on Pews? _____

Bridal party change in Parish Hall? _____   (Bridal Party assembles in Parish Hall 30 minutes before time set for wedding.

Number of Bridesmaids: _____   Number of Ushers: _____

Flowers: Name of Florist_____Phone Number:_____   Church bowls
           may go to the florist to be arranged.

           Time of delivery to church _____. Will flowers remain at the church?

           _____

Music: Bride and groom must contact church organist.

Candelabras:
      a. Two five-branch candelabras in sanctuary needed?_____
      b. Aisle wall candelabras needed? _____
      c. Both sanctuary and aisle candelabras needed? _____

NOTE: Altar and choir lights are always used. Nave lights used at couple's discretion.

Give copy of this sheet to bride and groom.

ABSOLUTELY NO PHOTOGRAPHY DURING CEREMONY!

Fig. 9–13
Example of Pre-Wedding Form

UNCTION

This sacrament is one that has been commonly, if mistakenly, called "Last Rites." It is certainly available to anyone who is ill physically, emotionally, or spiritually at any time, not just at the time of death. The service is found under Ministration to the Sick (pp. 453-461) in the Prayer Book.

Of ancient practice, James 5:13-16 shows continued use of this rite of healing for the sick with confession of sin, prayer, and anointing by the "presbyters of the church." The 1979 Book of Common Prayer provides for a Liturgy of the Word, the laying on of hands, with or without anointing, communion from the reserved sacrament, or a private celebration of the Eucharist with the sick person. It also provides for the laying on of hands or anointing at a public celebration of the Eucharist. A Public Service of Healing is also found in the Book of Occasional Services (pp. 147-154 in 1st edition; pp. 162-169 in 2nd edition).

Altar Guild Duties
The following additional responsibilities are typical for a public healing service.

TYPICAL ALTAR GUILD DUTIES FOR A HEALING SERVICE

1. On the side of the vesting table in the sacristy, set out white stole with strip of coronation material, the oil stock, a lavabo towel, the priest's healing booklet (which is marked with his or her name), booklets for servers who may be present, and the current prayer list.

2. See that the healing booklets are available at the back of the church.

Fig. 9–14
Example of Typical Altar Guild Healing Service Duties

The Burial of the Dead

The two services of the church through which most non-Episcopalians have contact with the church are weddings and funerals. Both rites are singularly beautiful and meaningful. However, it is the funerals which impress and sometimes startle visitors. The Liturgy for the Burial of the Dead is essentially an Easter Mass of the Resurrection.

It is a joyful liturgy with Easter music and white vestments and hangings marking the passage of a Christian into new birth. *"Life is changed, not ended."* The 1979 Book of Common Prayer provides rites in both traditional and contemporary language. Both are modeled on the Sunday Liturgy of Word and Sacrament and are part and parcel of a Eucharist celebrated in thanksgiving for the life of the deceased.

There is also a Burial Office when there is to be no Requiem Mass, and the Book of Occasional Services contains rites for one for whom the Prayer Book service is not appropriate (i.e., a non-Christian).

In addition to these services, we now have prayers to be used at a vigil and a rite for the reception of the body at the church (BCP pp. 466-467). For this service the paschal candle and pall should be in readiness at the door of the church.

Please note: The casket is closed before the service begins, whether at the funeral home or in the church, and is never re-opened.

Altar Guild Duties

Again, the altar guild's responsibilities will vary with parish tradition. Some altar guilds provide a reception in the parish hall following the service, for example. There is also a difference in your responsibilities if the funeral will include a Mass. The following figures are typical of duties of funerals and also of funerals that include a Requiem Mass.

TYPICAL ALTAR GUILD DUTIES FOR FUNERALS

1. See that RESERVED PARKING signs are set out in driveways early on the morning of funeral. Reserve parking spaces closest to main doors of the church for hearse and immediate family. Reserve front pews for immediate family of deceased.

2. Check flower arrangement in sanctuary area, if any. NO FLOWERS ON THE CASKET.

3. Altar is vested in white.

4. Set out white cope, stole, and white surplice for priest.

5. Set out and light the office lights.

6. Place the funeral pall on the back pew and indicate its presence to the undertaker. Be ready to assist the undertaker with the pall.

7. Place the bier candles, two on each side of the center aisle, level with the first pew. Indicate to pallbearers to move candles to the head and foot of the casket when it is in place.

8. Have holy water bucket and sprinkler available for priest.

9. Set out paschal candle in center aisle level with front pews if body is not present, otherwise in front of first step.

10. If body is not present, do not put out the bier candles.

11. Remove all Mass pamphlets from pews. Hand out Burial Office pamphlets. Be sure to pick up after the service and replace Mass pamphlets.

Fig. 9–15
Example of Typical Altar Guild Funeral Duties

TYPICAL ALTAR GUILD DUTIES FOR REQUIEM MASS

In addition to Items 1 through 11 from Figure 9-15:

1. Place two eucharistic candles on the altar, light at the time of Requiem Mass.

2. Set out eucharistic vestments (white). Priest may use at his or her discretion.

3. Set up vested chalice (using white), cruets, bread box, lavabo bowl and towel.

4. Hand out Requiem Mass pamphlets. Be sure to pick up afterwards.

5. Please remain in the church to make audible responses.

Fig. 9–16
Example of Typical Altar Guild Requiem Mass Duties

The Reconciliation of a Penitent (BCP pp. 446-452)
In the early church, penitence was a public affair and usually included discipline and excommunication. The practice of private penance developed later but was expected for matters of conscience known to the penitent and God alone, until eventually confession was required at least once a year.

The Anglican position was stated in the 1549 Prayer Book: Those who could not quiet their consciences through private prayer were to confess to a priest but shouldn't be offended if others did not require it.

The 1979 Book of Common Prayer provides several forms for the reconciliation of a penitent. It is important to remember that one confesses sin in order to be forgiven, not so that one may be punished.

Altar Guild Duties
Altar guild members have no responsibilities for this service since it is customarily private.

DAILY OFFICES

To this point in Module 9, we have assumed that the principal service of the church is the Eucharist and, therefore, it is the weekly form of service in most Episcopal churches in the U.S. However, many of our churches traditionally use Morning Prayer as the main service for most Sundays each month.

There is certainly historical precedent for a Morning Prayer service. Almost from the beginning of the church, the faithful have met for morning services that included prayers, psalms, songs, scripture, and instruction. Early monastic communities evolved a rather complicated routine of "offices" that marked their day. In the *Book of Hours*, which reached popularity in the fifteenth century, prayers used for the laity were associated with the life of the Virgin Mary:

- *Matins* could either be included with midnight or middle-of-the-night devotions – associated with the Annunciation.
- *Lauds* was for morning prayers – associated with the Visitation.
- *Prime* was to mark the first hour (6:00 A.M.), or the beginning of the day – associated with the Nativity.
- *Terce* corresponded to the third-hour division of the day, according to the Roman day (around 9:00 A.M.) – associated with the Annunciation to the Shepherds.
- *Sext* was for noontime prayer.
- *Nones* was prayer around 3:00 P.M. (or ninth-hour, for the Romans) – associated with the Presentation in the Temple.
- *Vespers* was for evening prayer – associated with the Flight into Egypt.
- *Compline* was traditionally the last service before bedtime, after which silence and fasting was kept – associated with the Coronation of the Virgin.

The morning and evening devotions (lauds and vespers) were the offices that became commonly used for public worship. However, during the Middle Ages, these too declined in popularity. In the first Prayer Book (in 1549), portions of matins, lauds and prime were combined to form a Morning Prayer service. Evening Prayer included parts of vespers and compline.

The 1979 BCP has both Morning and Evening Prayer services (in two versions each) that provide for a systematic reading of the psalms and scripture. In addition, the BCP also includes "An Order of Service for Noonday" and "An Order for Compline."

As a general rule, there are fewer preparations required from the altar guild for any of the daily offices. However, Figure 9–17 provides reminders of things that need to be considered. In many cases, preparations for Morning and Evening Prayer services are done by those responsible for conducting the services.

**TYPICAL ALTAR GUILD DUTIES
FOR MORNING OR EVENING PRAYER**

1. Depending on instructions, the altar dustcover may remain on the altar, or the fair linen may be replaced with another type of altar cover. Set out books for officiant and reader(s).

2. Clean and polish alms basins, torches, candlelighters/snuffers, and brass candle followers, etc. Check candles in office lights and torches to make certain they are sufficient to last through the service(s). Office lights may be lighted or not, as instructed. However, eucharistic lights are either not on the altar at all, or not lighted.

3. Flower arrangements may or may not be used in the sanctuary, depending on the season.

4. Dust and sweep narthex, nave and sanctuary. Generally pick up and straighten books and hymnals in nave.

**Fig. 9–17
Example of Typical Altar Guild Morning/Evening Prayer Duties**

OTHER SERVICES

There are other services and special liturgies that require some special consideration, and sometimes extra efforts on the part of the Altar Guild. The BCP (pp. 263 - 295) contains *Proper Liturgies for Special Days*:
*   Ash Wednesday
*   The Sunday of the Passion: Palm Sunday
*   Maundy Thursday
*   Good Friday
*   Holy Saturday
*   The Great Vigil of Easter

On the following pages, the figures provide reminders of typical Altar Guild considerations. Use each of the figures to develop a unique list of duties for your parish. Check with your rector or Altar Guild director to confirm and verify your list.

ASH WEDNESDAY

As stated earlier in this course, Ash Wednesday marks the beginning of Lent. The liturgy provided by the 1979 BCP includes the imposition of ashes, usually applied to the forehead in the form of a cross.

From an altar guild perspective, the service requires preparation of the ashes and some thought about protecting the linens from stains. In most cases, the ashes are derived by burning palms that were either leftover or returned by parishioners from the previous Palm Sunday. They may be burned in any safe fashion that you prefer (i.e., in a skillet or special container, set aside for the purpose). However, after burning them, they should be sifted through a strainer of some type to remove any large particles. Keep in mind that a small amount of sifted ashes goes a long way. The ashes should be placed in a small container on the credence table in the sanctuary for the service.

A helpful hint: Be sure to place a slice of white bread and slices of lemon on the credence table for the priest to clean the ashes from his or her fingers. After the imposition of ashes, having these items on the credence table will allow the celebrant to "cut" the ashes with the lemon slices and to absorb the residue with the bread. This will protect the lavabo towel, and is more effective than plain water.

TYPICAL ALTAR GUILD DUTIES FOR ASH WEDNESDAY

Set up for a eucharistic service as usual. In addition, the following should be set-out:

1.   Place container holding ashes on credence table in sanctuary.

2.   Place two slices of fresh lemon and a slice of white bread in a dish on the credence table.

3.   Also, place an extra lavabo towel on the credence table.

Fig. 9–18
Example of Typical Altar Guild Ash Wednesday Duties

THE SUNDAY OF THE PASSION: PALM SUNDAY

The custom of a procession marking the triumphal entry of our Lord into Jerusalem dates from the early centuries of the church. These processions featured the singing of psalms (especially Psalm 118), and the carrying of palm fronds. The 1979 BCP restored the procession as part of the liturgy of the day, usually preceding a Eucharist.

Since Palm Sunday is at the end of the penitential season of Lent (when flowers are normally not used), it is also the first time during that period that plants are introduced into the sanctuary. These usually take the form of either palm plants or palm fronds, arranged in the sanctuary and even attached to the processional cross. Arrangements of large fan-palm fronds look very good, if the "hairy" strings and dead ends are trimmed.

In addition to sanctuary decorations, individual palm leaves are usually blessed and presented to each member of the congregation. For a while, the use of palm leaves that had been folded into small crosses was a popular method of distributing the palms. However, this is becoming more rare because some feel that the symbolism of carrying the palm is lost with the small, folded cross.

Regardless of the mode of presentation of the palms, or the amount of palms used in the sanctuary, they should be ordered in advance – unless, of course, your parish is in an area where palms are plentiful. In some cases, palms are neither available locally, nor affordable. If this is the circumstance in your parish, check with your rector about alternatives.

Figure 9–19 provides typical things for the altar guild to consider in preparation for Palm Sunday.

TYPICAL ALTAR GUILD DUTIES FOR PALM SUNDAY

Frontal and vestments are passion (dark) red. If full solemn set is available, place the dalmatic and tunicle out, also.

1. Place palm crosses and palm fronds in wicker baskets. Divide the supply appropriately between the services. Place on small table.

2. Decorate the sanctuary with palms.

3. Unveil the processional cross and decorate with palm fronds.

4. Have a small table available (with credence table cloth) for the blessing of the palms.

5. Place a Holy Water bucket on the credence table.

6. Place the gold Gospel Book on the altar. Place the plain Gospel Book on the pulpit.

7. The acolyte will carry the palm crosses to the narthex following the service.

8. Make sure that the congregation's leaflets for the Passion are placed in the narthex to be handed-out.

Fig. 9–19
Example of Typical Altar Guild Palm Sunday Duties

MAUNDY THURSDAY

In the previous module, we discussed the fact that the Maundy Thursday liturgy commemorates the institution of the Eucharist. This is a "celebration," in contrast to the penitential atmosphere of Lent. In other words, there are flowers in the sanctuary, and glorias are said or sung.

In addition, the liturgy allows for a ceremony of washing feet that, if done, follows the Gospel and homily. If this is a custom in your parish, the altar guild is responsible for providing the materials required for the ceremony (i.e., footwashing pan, water, washcloth, towel, etc.).

If Good Friday services are to include communion from the reserved Sacrament, the extra Sacrament that is to be used is consecrated during the Maundy Thursday service. At the end of the Eucharist, the Sacrament is removed (in many parishes) in procession to an Altar of Repose. The altar guild is responsible for setting up the Altar of Repose in advance. Check with your altar guild director or your rector for how and where this is normally done.

In most churches the Eucharist is followed by the ceremonial stripping of the altar, where all candles, linen, flowers, vessels, etc., are removed from the sanctuary and the altar is washed down. The altar guild is expected to provide the materials for washing down the altar, and may or may not be involved in stripping the sanctuary. At the very least, someone from the altar guild should be stationed in the sacristy to direct servers who are removing the vessels, candles, etc. Rather than chaos, this should be a solemn, orderly ceremony, with everything being placed in its proper cabinet or cupboard.

In some instances, where the crosses and shrine figures in the sanctuary and nave are *not* shrouded during Lent, they may be shrouded as a part of the Maundy Thursday service. If this is custom in your parish, the shrouds and ties should be available just inside the sacristy.

At the end of this final activity, the people of the congregation usually depart without instruction, music, or ceremony. In many parishes, a prayer watch before the altar of repose is kept from the end of Maundy Thurday service until the Good Friday liturgy. The altar guild may be asked to prepare a sign-up sheet several weeks in advance, to post in the narthex or parish hall, so that members of the parish may select their preferred watch times.

Figure 9–20 provides a list of typical altar guild activities for Maundy Thursday.

TYPICAL ALTAR GUILD DUTIES FOR MAUNDY THURSDAY

In addition to usual eucharistic set-up:

1.   Prepare the Altar of Repose.

2.   Prepare floral arrangements for the sanctuary.

3.   Prepare water, footwashing pan, wash cloth and towel(s) (If required for the washing of feet ceremony).

4.   Have humeral veil(s) available (if appropriate) for procession to Altar of Repose.

5.   Assign altar guild member to direct traffic in sacristy as items are removed from sanctuary.

6.   Set out shrouds for crosses and shrine figures (if appropriate).

Fig. 9–20
Example of Typical Altar Guild Maundy Thursday Duties

GOOD FRIDAY

Historically, the veneration of the cross dates to the early church at Jerusalem, where they brought-out what was thought to be the true cross and presented it for veneration at the place where Jesus was crucified.

(Several years ago, a member of the Order of the Holy Cross (OHC), an Episcopal monastic order, displayed for the author a splinter of the "true cross" with an ancient certification from a bishop (of some distant century) as to its authenticity. When asked if it was really a splinter of the cross, the response was, "Well, we have a certification from a bishop that says it is. On the other hand, we do *not* have a certification from anyone that it is not!")

The liturgy provided by the 1979 BCP is a moving and beautiful service. However, individual parish custom will vary as to its implementation. The altar guild will be responsible for providing any linen required for communion from the Reserved Sacrament. Also, frequently a special cross or crucifix is used for this service, so the altar guild is responsible for making that available.

HOLY SATURDAY

There is no Eucharist celebrated on this day, so, altar guild duties are minimal for the Holy Saturday liturgy. That does not imply that there are no duties for the guild on the day itself. After the liturgy, there is much activity in preparation for the Great Vigil of Easter.

Figure 9–21 provides a list of typical duties in preparation for the Great Vigil and Easter.

TYPICAL ALTAR GUILD DUTIES FOR
THE GREAT VIGIL OF EASTER

In addition to usual eucharistic set-up:

1. Remove shrouds from crosses and shrine figures in sanctuary and nave.

2. Set-up frontals, altar linen, candles, torches, processional cross, banners, etc. (If parish has a tabernacle or aumbry leave door open.)

3. Prepare and arrange special floral arrangements for the sanctuary.

4. Have a candelabra stationed near the litany desk.

5. Prepare and set out (in narthex) tapers with cardboard holders.

6. Set out vessels for any baptisms.

7. Set out materials for the lighting of the "new fire." (A hibachi on some type of non-flamable surface works well.)

8. Set out the new paschal candle near the "new fire" set-up.

9. Set out extra bulletins, and make sure there is extra wine and wafers. (This is true of Easter Sunday's services too! Your bi-annual parishioners will attend one of these services.)

Fig. 9–21
Example of Typical Altar Guild Duties
Before the Great Vigil of Easter

EPISCOPAL SERVICES

They are called *episcopal services* because the bishop is present and is almost always (if not always) the principal celebrant. They include all ordinations (BCP pp. 510-555), the Celebration of a New Ministry (pp. 558-565), the Dedication and Consecration of a Church (pp. 566-579) and the bishop's visitation. The focus of all of these rites is always the Holy Eucharist.

The Ordination of a Bishop, Priest, or Deacon

The *Apostolic Tradition* of Hippolytus, dating about A.D. 215, contains the earliest text of ordination rites available to us. In those rites, a bishop was ordained by several bishops who laid hands on his head. One of them said a prayer which stated the ministry of a bishop, the new bishop was greeted with the kiss of peace and then presided at the celebration of Eucharist.

Only the bishop laid hands on a new deacon since the deacon was directly responsible to him. When a priest was ordained, other priests joined the bishop in the laying on of hands since the ordinand was entering a corporate body presided over by the bishop.

In either case, ordination to the diaconate or priesthood, the prayers described the ministry of the order and the newly ordained functioned appropriately at the Eucharist which followed. The deacon prepared the altar and administered communion. The new priest stood with the bishop and other priests during the eucharistic prayers and joined in the breaking of the bread.

This is essentially the pattern followed today, with the addresses, examination, and prayers of consecration describing and depicting more clearly the order being conferred.

Altar Guild Duties During Episcopal Visitations

In most parishes a visit by the bishop calls for putting one's best foot forward. Just remember, the bishop is the head of the "Episcopal" Church, so the altar guild stands in readiness to do whatever the bishop asks.

A small extra candle may be placed on the altar in honor of the bishop's presence. (A scented candle is always nice to air the place out!) The bishop's chair is placed in the sanctuary. Otherwise, just function as usual.

THE BOOK OF OCCASIONAL SERVICES

The Book of Occasional Services is a compendium of optional rites which supplement the Book of Common Prayer. It was issued with the approval of the General Convention of 1979. None of the rites contained is mandatory and it is not likely that all congregations may find use for some of the services even occasionally. If one of the services is used, a preparatory general meeting of the clergy, musicians, acolytes and other lay assistants, and a member of the altar guild will be most helpful to all concerned.

The Table of Contents first lists things appropriate to various seasons of the church year, such as Advent and the Advent Wreath, an Advent Festival of Lessons and Music, Vigil for Christmas Eve, Station at a Christmas Creche, Christmas Festival of Lessons and Music, Services for New Year's Eve, Blessing in Homes at Epiphany, Candlemass Procession, The Way of the Cross, Tenebrae, Agape for Maundy Thursday, Rogation Procession, Vigil for the Eve of All Saints' Day, and Service for All Hallows' Eve.

Next are the Pastoral Services such as Preparation of Adults for Holy Baptism, Celebration for a Home, Anniversary of a Marriage, Public Service of Healing, Burial of One Who Does Not Profess the Christian Faith, and Commissioning for Lay Ministries in the Church (such as altar guild members, acolytes, Sunday School teachers, choir members, layreaders, etc).

Following these are forms for the Dedication of Church Furnishings and Ornaments (altar, font, chalice and patens, bell, cross, candlesticks, altar cloths and hangings, Gospel Book, Bible, lectionary, and vestments), Groundbreaking for a Church, Laying of a Cornerstone, even a Restoring of Things Profaned and Secularizing a Consecrated Building.

The Episcopal services, all of which culminate in the celebration of Eucharist include: Reaffirmation of Ordination Vows, Recognition and Investiture of a Diocesan Bishop, Welcoming and Seating of a Bishop in the Cathedral, and Setting Apart for a Special Vocation, such as admission to the noviatiate (set within a Daily Office) and the taking of temporary or annual vows and final or life vows. Also in the Book of Occasional Services are various anthems and blessings for special occasions.

Most of the time, the clergy will be as much in the dark about the conduct of these services as the altar guild is, since they are used so seldom. Therefore, it is very important that there be a meeting of the minds in the planning of them so that they are beautiful offerings of worship.

SUMMARY

The Episcopal church teaches and provides for seven sacraments:
Two Dominical Sacraments:
- Baptism
- Holy Communion

Five lessor or minor sacraments:
- Holy Confirmation
- Holy Matrimony
- Holy Orders
- Penance
- Holy Unction

Baptism is the most important event in the life of a Christian. The 1979 BCP stresses that baptism is to be reserved for Easter, Pentecost, the Feast of the Baptism of our Lord, All Saints' Day or the Sunday following, and the bishop's visitation. Otherwise the rites are to be administered at a principal Eucharist on a Sunday or other feast. "Private" baptisms are not provided for, except in the case of dire emergency, when any Christian may baptize anywhere at any time.

The Holy Eucharist is the principal act of worship on the Lord's Day and other major feasts. The Holy Eucharist is an outward and visible sign of the inward and invisible Presence of Christ. It is also symbolic of what our Lord, out of love for us, was willing to do for us.

The pastoral offices, which include the five lesser sacraments, are designed and intended to be celebrated in conjunction with the Holy Eucharist. They include:

- **Confirmation** – A Eucharist with the bishop as celebrant follows confirmations that are separate from baptisms. The color is red for confirmations and white if there are also baptisms.

- **Weddings** – The New Testament contains no information about a Christian marriage ritual. The BCP sets the rite in context of the Liturgy of the Word and Sacrament. It also provides the Blessing of a Civil Marriage and An Order for Marriage. The Book of Occasional Services has a rite for the Anniversary of a Marriage.

- **Unction** – Mistakenly called "Last Rites," this sacrament is available to anyone who is ill physically, emotionally, or spiritually at any time, not just at the time of death.

- **The Burial of the Dead** – The Liturgy for the Burial of the Dead is essentially an Easter Mass of the Resurrection. It is joyful, with Easter music and white vestments and hangings marking the passage of a Christian into new birth.

- **The Reconciliation of a Penitent** – The 1979 Book of Common Prayer provides several forms for the reconciliation of a penitent. It is important to remember that one confesses sin in order to be forgiven, not so that one may be punished.

Morning and Evening Prayer services are found in the BCP, as well as Proper Liturgies for Special Days, including:
- Ash Wednesday
- Palm Sunday
- Maundy Thursday
- Good Friday
- Holy Saturday

Episcopal Services are so called because the bishop is present and almost always the principal celebrant. The focus of all of these rites is always the Holy Eucharist.

In apostolic tradition, a bishop is ordained by several bishops who lay hands on his head. One of them says a prayer which states the ministry of a bishop, the new bishop is greeted with the kiss of peace and then presides at the celebration of Eucharist. Only the bishop lays hands on a new deacon since the deacon is directly responsible to him or her. When a priest is ordained, other priests join the bishop in the laying on of hands since the new priest is entering a corporate body presided over by the bishop.

A visit by the bishop is special but requires minimal special activities. The altar guild should stand in readiness to do whatever the bishop asks. A small extra candle may be placed on the altar in honor of the bishop's presence. Otherwise, just function as usual.

The Book of Occasional Services contains optional rites which supplement the Book of Common Prayer. None of the rites contained are mandatory. If one of the services is used, a preparatory general meeting of the clergy, musicians, acolytes and other lay assistants and a member of the altar guild, will be most helpful to all concerned.

If you feel comfortable with the information contained in Module 9, proceed to the progress check. If not, you may wish to review the module again before completing the progress check.

MODULE 9
PROGRESS CHECK

Respond to the questions by filling in the blanks. Feel free to use the text of the module to assist you in answering.

1. The two Dominical Sacraments are:

   _____

   _____

2. The five lesser or minor sacraments are:

   _____

   _____

   _____

   _____

   _____

3. The _____ is the principal act of worship on the Lord's Day and other major feasts.

4. The three types of eucharistic services (as listed in this module) are:

   _____

   _____

   _____

5. The _____ contains optional rites which supplement the Book of Common Prayer.

(ANSWERS ON THE BACK OF THIS PAGE)

MODULE 9
ANSWER SHEET

Respond to the questions by filling in the blanks. Feel free to use the text of the module to assist you in answering.

1. The two Dominical Sacraments are:
    Baptism
    Holy Communion

2. The five lesser or minor sacraments are:
    Holy Confirmation
    Holy Matrimony
    Holy Orders
    Penance
    Holy Unction

3. The **Holy Eucharist** is the principal act of worship on the Lord's Day and other major feasts.

4. The three types of eucharistic services (as listed in this module) are:

    Low Mass
    Family Mass
    Solemn High Mass

5. The **Book of Occasional Services** contains optional rites which supplement the Book of Common Prayer.

Now, look over your answers. If you feel comfortable that you understand the material in Module 9, please continue to Module 10. If not, you may wish to review the material again.

MODULE 10
THE SACRISTY

A backstage job requires some organization. It would be confusing to have the lights in the wardrobe room, or the small props out in the orchestra pit. Likewise, it is vital that the passion play's backstage crew know where the props (large and small) are kept.

TIME:
Approximately 15 minutes

OBJECTIVE:
Given the contents of Module 10, you will be able to demonstrate an understanding of the cleaning required prior to services by responding to simple fill-in-the-blank questions with 100% accuracy.

ACTIVITIES:
- Read the text of the module
- Complete Exercises

MATERIAL REQUIRED:
- This Module
- Pen or Pencil
- Progress Check

OTHER RESOURCE MATERIAL:
Contents of your sacristy.

COURSE MAP

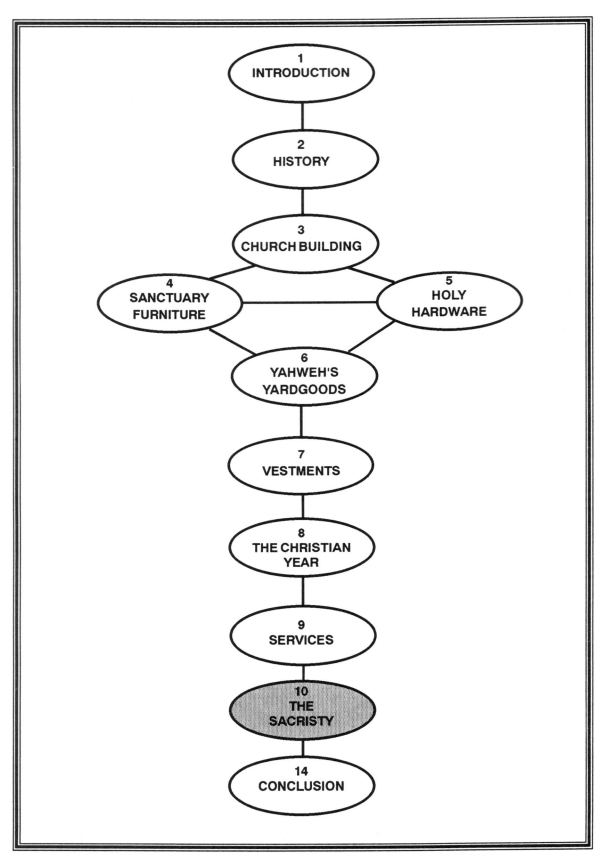

MODULE 10
THE SACRISTY

INTRODUCTION

As noted in the previous module, there needs to be an order to the work of the sacristy. The order that results from the consistency of performance that the check-off lists you have created will help.

But, order extends into the cabinets, drawers, and closets of the sacristy as well. Everyone on an altar guild team should know where everything is kept in this vital workroom. When vessels, linens, and vestments have been used and are ready to put away, they should be returned to their assigned place. Otherwise, half (or more) of the next team's time will be spent looking for what they need.

Remember, we are attempting to make the job easier, not practicing for an Easter egg hunt!

Most of the time you will work together with several others in the preparation for services, although an occasion may arise when you may have to work by yourself. It is vital that you know where things are kept. With knowledge comes power! Therefore, knowing what to do and where things are kept will prevent solo service from becoming a scary proposition.

Like the exercises that you did in the module on church buildings, the following exercises are designed to cause you to investigate your sacristy — or sacristies, in some cases. So, they are far more than "busywork." When you complete each exercise, check your responses with your altar guild director or your rector.

EXERCISE 10–1
IDENTIFYING SACRISTY SPACE

Use this page to draw an outline of *your* sacristy. Since each building is different, identify the cabinets, closets, doors, and vesting areas as they apply to your facilities. Don't worry about the quality of your drawing (no one is going to see it, except you). For the best result, you should go into the sacristy to complete this exercise. Sometimes drawing from memory results in forgotten, or out-of-proportion items. Figure 10–1 provides an example of a sacristy floor plan.

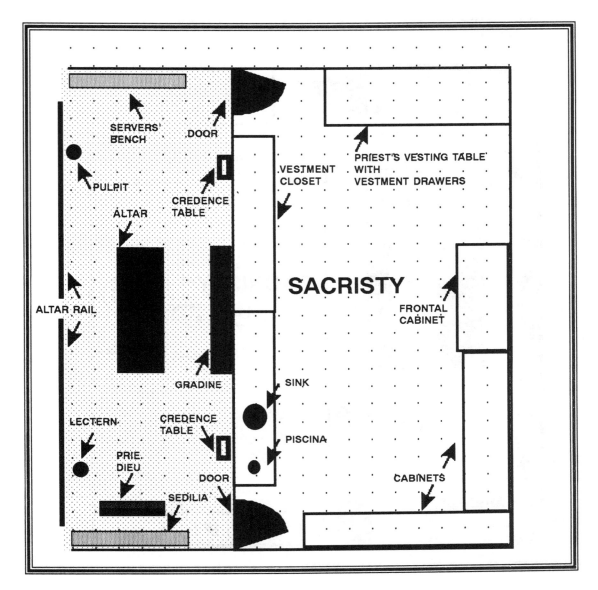

Fig. 10–1
Example of Sacristy Layout

Your sacristy may, in fact, be a series of rooms. But it is likely that it – or they – will be located somewhere in close proximity to the altar and the sanctuary area. If you have more than one room for your sacristy, make copies of Exercise 10–1 and draw in the layout for each room. Be sure to identify each closet, each cabinet, each counter, etc. It will be important to the other exercises in this module.

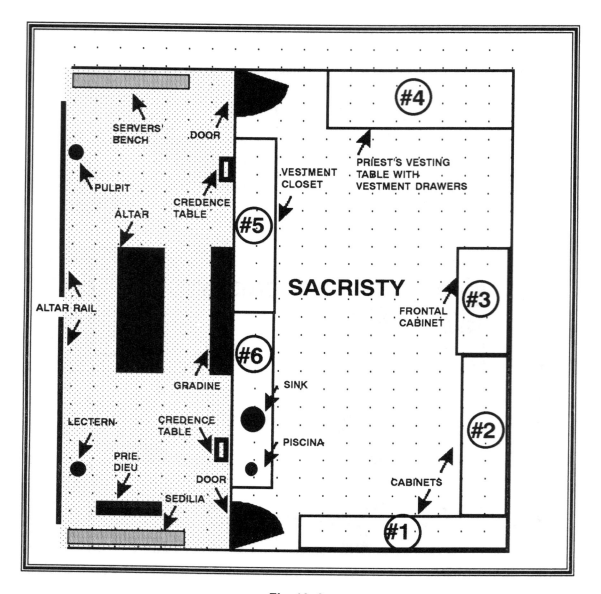

Fig. 10–2
Example of Numbering Cabinets, Closets, Counters

Using your Exercise 10–1 drawing, identify each cabinet, closet, and counter by numbering each. Figure 10–2 (above) provides an example of how to number each item.

EXERCISE 10–2
IDENTIFYING CABINET(S) AND CONTENTS

Use this page to draw an outline of each individual cabinet, closet or cupboard. Identify each item by the number that you gave it in your Exercise 10–1 drawing. When you have drawn the item, identify the contents. Figures 10–3, 10–4, 10–5, 10–6, 10–7, and 10–8 provide examples of cabinets, cupboards, drawers, and closets identified by their contents. Copy this page as many times as needed to complete the exercise for each of your numbered items. Note: The only way to be sure about the contents is to inventory each PERSONALLY.

ITEM #_____

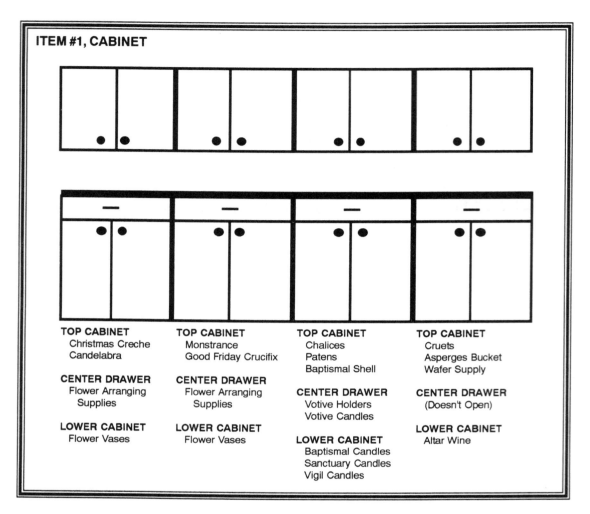

ITEM #1, CABINET

TOP CABINET
Christmas Creche
Candelabra

CENTER DRAWER
Flower Arranging
   Supplies

LOWER CABINET
Flower Vases

TOP CABINET
Monstrance
Good Friday Crucifix

CENTER DRAWER
Flower Arranging
   Supplies

LOWER CABINET
Flower Vases

TOP CABINET
Chalices
Patens
Baptismal Shell

CENTER DRAWER
Votive Holders
Votive Candles

LOWER CABINET
Baptismal Candles
Sanctuary Candles
Vigil Candles

TOP CABINET
Cruets
Asperges Bucket
Wafer Supply

CENTER DRAWER
(Doesn't Open)

LOWER CABINET
Altar Wine

Fig. 10–3
Example of Item #1 Cabinet and Contents

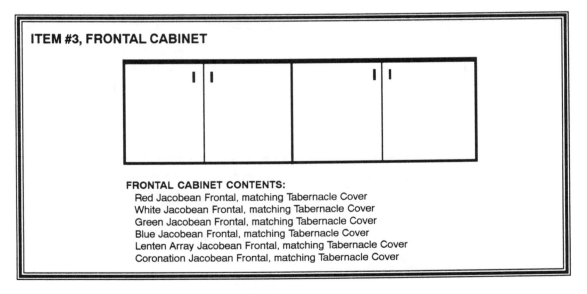

ITEM #2, CABINET

TOP DRAWER
Baptismal Towels
Purificators
Lavabo Towels

DRAWER #2
Corporals
Palls

DRAWER #3
Credence Table
Cloths

BOTTOM DRAWER
Fair Linen

TOP DRAWER
Special Linen
Advent
Nativity
Lent

DRAWER #2
Altar Dust Covers

DRAWER #3
Confirmation Veils

BOTTOM DRAWER
Vestment Material
Scraps

TOP DRAWER
Special Linen
Ascension
Pentecost
Trinity

DRAWER #2
Vestment Table
Dust Covers

DRAWER #3
Sacristy Towels

BOTTOM DRAWER
Wedding Bows

Fig. 10–4
Example of Item #2 Cabinet Drawer Contents

ITEM #3, FRONTAL CABINET

FRONTAL CABINET CONTENTS:
Red Jacobean Frontal, matching Tabernacle Cover
White Jacobean Frontal, matching Tabernacle Cover
Green Jacobean Frontal, matching Tabernacle Cover
Blue Jacobean Frontal, matching Tabernacle Cover
Lenten Array Jacobean Frontal, matching Tabernacle Cover
Coronation Jacobean Frontal, matching Tabernacle Cover

Fig. 10–5
Example of Item #3 Frontal Cabinet

ITEM #4, PRIEST'S VESTING TABLE

—	WHITE	—	—	RED	—
—	GREEN	—	—	BLUE	—
—	CORONATION	—	—	LENTEN ARRAY	—
—	PURPLE	—	—	GOLD	—
—	MULTICOLOR	—	—	ROSE	—
—		—	—		—
—		—	—		—
—		—	—		—

PRIEST'S VESTING CABINET
Top of cabinet used to set out vestments (chasuble, stole, girdle).
Top of cabinet also used for Gospel Book, Bibles, Altar Books, etc.
Cabinet drawers contain burse, veil, extra stoles, etc., of the color
   indicated.
Bottom drawers contain shrouds used during Lent.

Fig. 10–6
Example of Item #4 Priest's Vesting Cabinet

ITEM #5, VESTMENT CLOSET

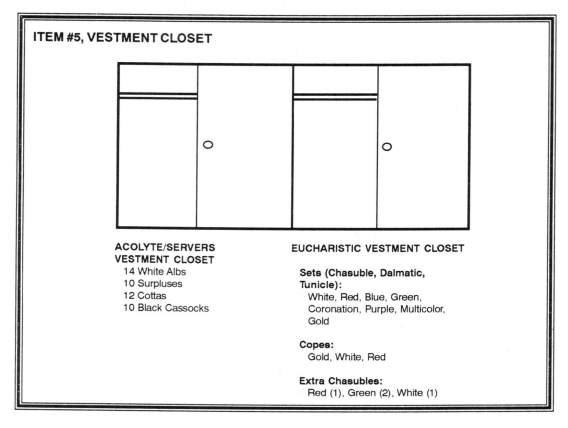

ACOLYTE/SERVERS
VESTMENT CLOSET
   14 White Albs
   10 Surpluses
   12 Cottas
   10 Black Cassocks

EUCHARISTIC VESTMENT CLOSET

Sets (Chasuble, Dalmatic,
Tunicle):
   White, Red, Blue, Green,
   Coronation, Purple, Multicolor,
   Gold

Copes:
   Gold, White, Red

Extra Chasubles:
   Red (1), Green (2), White (1)

Fig. 10–7
Example of Item #5 Vestment Closet

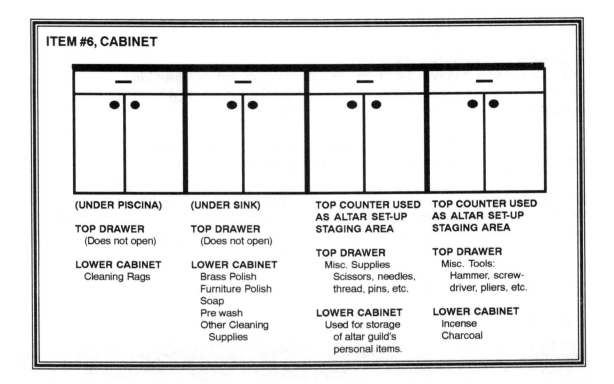

ITEM #6, CABINET

| (UNDER PISCINA) | (UNDER SINK) | TOP COUNTER USED AS ALTAR SET-UP STAGING AREA | TOP COUNTER USED AS ALTAR SET-UP STAGING AREA |

TOP DRAWER
(Does not open)

TOP DRAWER
(Does not open)

TOP DRAWER
Misc. Supplies
  Scissors, needles,
  thread, pins, etc.

TOP DRAWER
Misc. Tools:
  Hammer, screw-
  driver, pliers, etc.

LOWER CABINET
Cleaning Rags

LOWER CABINET
Brass Polish
Furniture Polish
Soap
Pre wash
Other Cleaning
  Supplies

LOWER CABINET
Used for storage
  of altar guild's
  personal items.

LOWER CABINET
Incense
Charcoal

Fig. 10–8
Example of Item #6 Cleaning Supplies Cabinet

Well, that was quite an exercise! Perhaps we should shout, **"Can we have your attention, please!"** However, if you were thorough in your efforts, you now know where everything in your sacristy is located.

That was certainly the prime purpose of Exercise 10–2. However, a secondary benefit of the exercise is that you now have the beginnings of a complete inventory of your sacristy's contents.

INVENTORIES
Probably one of the most important things for an altar guild to do is to keep a running inventory of altar linens of every type, vestments, vessels, vases, candlesticks, incense pots, and any and all ecclesiastical accoutrements of whatever type.

The reasons for this are many: one is simply to keep track of things. Another is for insurance purposes. Yet another is to establish a "Wish List" for memorial gifts.

LAUNDRY CHECKLIST

(You have worked very hard during this module, so we will not make this into an exercise. However, you may wish to make such a check-off list, if your altar guild does not already have one.)

Another checklist that you will find absolutely essential for everyone's peace of mind is a sign-up sheet for linens taken to be laundered.

Nothing is more frustrating (read "infuriating") than to arrive for altar guild work only to find that some kind souls have taken all the linens to launder but haven't returned them. Therefore, it is well, if one does take linens home to launder, to "do-them-up" at once and return them at the earliest opportunity.

A linen check-out list (posted in the sacristy) might look something like this:

SACRISTY LINENS

FAIR LINEN	ALBS	TOWELS	AMICES	OTHER	DATE TAKEN	BY WHOM	DATE RETURNED

Figure 10-9
Example of Linen Check-Out Sheet

FLOWER CHART

In some parishes the altar guild is in charge of the flower chart. In others, that is done by the parish secretary. Whoever has the responsibility for that part of it – signing people up for various services and handling the finances of it – it is the altar guild's responsibility to see that appropriate flowers are in the sanctuary in season and out of season (except for those church seasons when flowers aren't used, i.e., Lent). Flower charts may be purchased from almost any place that supplies other forms used by the church.

CLEANING SUPPLIES

Someone must be in charge of seeing that cleaning supplies are always on hand before the items are used up. Post a "Cleaning Supplies Needed" list in the sacristy for the person in charge, and add items to the list when you notice a particular supply is running low.

ORDERING SUPPLIES

In general, someone must be in charge of all ordering. The emphasis is on the word "some<u>one</u>." It is a disaster to have four or five people ordering things. The result is not only a five-year supply of priest's wafers, but by ordering piecemeal, your parish pays excess shipping charges. Develop a system of maintaining a running inventory of all items that are used on a continuing basis, determining the level that will "trigger" an order for each.

This method is used by businesses to maintain their inventory efficiently. And, after all, that's what we in the altar guild are all about, isn't it? The Lord's business.

SPECIAL SERVICES

A very helpful form is one dealing with a "special" or "occasional" service. It is usually filled in at a meeting with the clergy staff and organist by an altar guild member in attendance and passed on to the team, and person (or persons) involved.

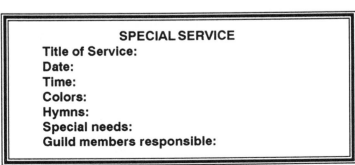

SPECIAL SERVICE
Title of Service:
Date:
Time:
Colors:
Hymns:
Special needs:
Guild members responsible:

Figure 10-10
Example of Special Service Sheet

ASK QUESTIONS

Ask if your parish has an inventory. If so, who is in charge of it? When was the last time it was updated? If your parish does not have an inventory sheet, volunteer to assist in preparing one, and post it in the sacristy.

Also, ask who is in charge of the flower chart, or flower calendar, at your parish. Determine where it is posted, and check it over to determine if there are any special memorial or thanksgiving floral gifts scheduled for weeks that you are on duty. Ask your altar guild director, or clergy about parish policy regarding flowers.

SUMMARY

The summary for this module is simply to look back over each of the pages that you created in your Exercises 10–1 and 10–2.

If you feel comfortable with the thoroughness of your efforts, proceed to the final module. If not, you may wish to revise your drawings (or the way they are labeled before proceeding to the final module. There is no progress check for this module. (Surprised? Well, you deserve a break.)

**MODULE 11
CONCLUSION
OR
*"SO THERE YOU HAVE IT"***

*If this were a movie – especially an animated one – we might
say, "That's all, folks!" But, this is really just the beginning.*

TIME:
Approximately 20 minutes

OBJECTIVE:
Given the contents of Module 11, you will be able to demonstrate an understanding of miscellaneous altar guild related information that is covered in this module (because the information does not fall conveniently into any of the other modules) by completing a fill-in-the-blank progress check with 100% accuracy.

ACTIVITIES:
- Read the text of the module
- Complete the Progress Check

MATERIAL REQUIRED:
- This Module
- Pen or Pencil
- Progress Check

OTHER RESOURCE MATERIAL:
None

COURSE MAP

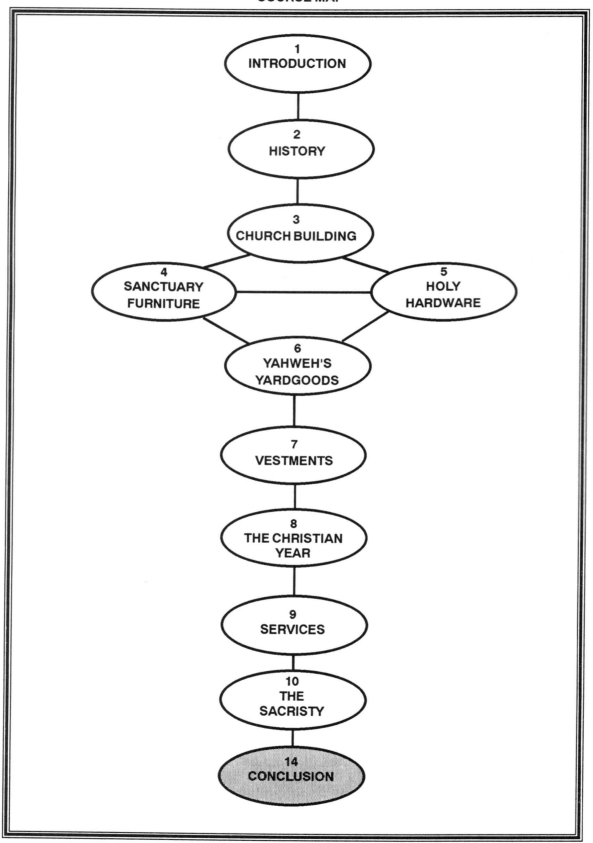

MODULE 11
CONCLUSION
OR
"SO THERE YOU HAVE IT"

INTRODUCTION

This module will cover a variety of subjects that either didn't fit conveniently into other modules, or subjects that if brought up at their associated time might have proved a little confusing.

HOLY HOUSEWORK

None of the holy housework is very glamorous, but it's necessary to keep the house of the Lord clean and orderly. Your particular situation may call for different ways of doing things, and that's fine. Determine what's best for you and set up your own work routine.

But whatever you do, and however you decide to do it, set up check lists of what is to be done for every kind of service. This seemingly time-consuming task will pay huge dividends in the long run: in time saved, nerves soothed, and mistakes (due to memory loss) largely eliminated.

YOUR MINISTRY

Think of your work as a ministry, as indeed it is! The beauty of the liturgies of the Episcopal Church are designed to provide meaningful worship. It is our ministry, in the altar guild, to help provide a *"worship-full"* environment for those who participate in each service – including ourselves.

Since appointment to the Altar Guild at your parish is not appointment to a full-time vocation, your service (however much time, however much effort) is a gift to God and your parish community. Try to think of it with the same spirit of giving that you would if you were preparing a Thanksgiving meal for a needy family in your town. That is, in fact, what you are doing. Every time the eucharistic meal is celebrated, there are people present who are in need – in need of Christ in their lives. Your efforts in the sacristy help bring him to them in a very real way.

So, regardless of whether you can afford a wealth or a "widow's mite" of your time and talents, give what you can to the glory of God and offer it as your gift and ministry.

FLOWERS

In recent times we have become accustomed to seeing flowers on or about the altar almost every Sunday except during Lent. That wasn't always the case. Flowers might be given in thanksgiving or as a special offering occasionally, but before 1930, flowers appeared less frequently.

Today, it is customary for members of the church to provide flowers for Sunday and other feasts, in thanksgiving or as memorials. Flowers for weddings are provided by the bride's family; funeral flowers are given by the family or close friends of the deceased; those for other occasions are a matter of decision by the clergy or worship committee.

Flowers should highlight the meaning of the day in color and arrangement. They should not dominate the space, interfere with movement, or otherwise call undue attention to themselves.

There are several schools of thought concerning by whom flowers should be arranged. Some churches use flowers donated by members from their gardens, or bought and arranged by a guild member gifted in flower arranging. Other parishes, through arrangements with a local florist, have flowers delivered ready to be put into their own containers. And that is fine, provided the florist understands the desired effect, the occasion, and the colors to be used.

Some churches use blooming potted plants occasionaly, instead of cut flowers. After their use in the church, they may be planted around the church property or given away. What happens to the flowers following service is the concern of the clergy. Frequently, they are sent or taken to the sick or shut-ins, to nursing homes or to some institution.

In selecting altar flowers, consideration should be given to the fact that some flowers have particular significance for special seasons:

> **Christmas:** holly, ivy, poinsettia, Christmas Rose, and/or other flowers that enhance these
>
> **Passiontide:** greens, palms, flowering branches
>
> **Easter:** lily, and/or other spring flowers

Remember that God's world is full of color and that white is the presence of all colors. However, keep in mind that locale, cost, and the availability of flowers may dictate the flowers used.

Perhaps no other single issue can cause contention more quickly than the uses of flowers for weddings or funerals, or where flowers may or may not be placed.

WEDDING FLOWERS

Let it be clearly understood, at the outset, that no bridal consultant dictates the use of flowers (or anything else!) in any wedding taking place in the Church. Quite the opposite is true. The consultant must work within the guidelines of the parish. That should be made clear to the bride in the initial consultation about the wedding.

The altar guild person interviewing the bride should point out the options available or ask preference. If there is any doubt, consult the clergy. In any case, if the altar is not used – as in a Nuptial Mass, it is NEVER to be blanketed with flowers or be set with huge vases. The altar is never a flower shelf!

Nor should the sanctuary be so cluttered with potted palms that it looks as though Tarzan and Jane were exchanging vows. If your parish doesn't have a set policy, ask the clergy for definite guidelines.

Flowers are never placed in or on the font. Around the base, yes, but nowhere else.

FUNERAL FLOWERS

The Episcopal Church has a policy concerning flowers at funerals. Only the flowers normally used at a Sunday Eucharist are allowed in the church at a funeral. Flowers delivered to the church may be placed in the sacristy to be given to the family after the service. If the casket arrives with a blanket of flowers over it, or a spray on it, they are removed and left outside the church to be replaced with the funeral pall when the remains are brought into the church.

The reasons for this are simple: We are all the same in the eyes of God; therefore the burial services are the same, *"high and low, rich and poor, one with another"* as the psalm says. (The same theology prevails in the use of the funeral pall. It doesn't matter if the casket is hammered bronze or a wooden box, worldly wealth or social status is simply not a consideration.)

LIGHTING CANDLES

Occasionaly, the Altar Guild person on duty is called upon to light the candles before the service and extinguish them following the service. In that event, the following illustrations provide the recommended order for this to be done.

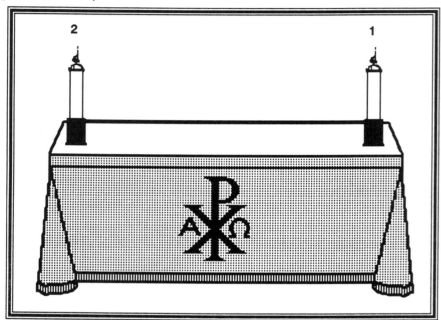

Fig. 11–1
Order of Lighting Eucharistic Candles

Fig. 11–2
Order of Extinguishing Eucharistic Candles

Fig. 11–3
Order of Lighting Office Candles

Fig. 11–4
Order of Extinguishing Office Candles

MEMORIALS

Every parish has various items (vestments, vessels, candlesticks, etc.) that have been given to the church as memorials. There should be a record somewhere in the parish office of the origin of these items. They were given to the glory of God and in loving memory of someone. As long as they are being used in God's service, they are indeed a fitting memorial.

However, because of time, change in church decor, etc., occasionally these items get shoved to the back of closets and cupboards, never to be used again. One of the things that should be done (as you inventory your sacristy) is to identify such items and, after checking with the rector (and perhaps the donor), give them to a mission or parish that needs them. Memorials that are never used are *not* memorials. Neither are they being used to the glory of God.

CONCLUDING STATEMENTS

We hope that in the course of this study we have been able to assure you that being or becoming a member of the altar guild is not as difficult as you may have thought. And we hope we have been able to dispel some of your anxiety.

As you become more and more familiar with preparation for services you will note that everything done follows a logical pattern. Believe it or not, you will soon settle into the joy of the work and each thing you do will become a prayer.

The sacristy and the time you spend there will become a very important part of your life. A dear, veteran altar guild member said once, "I dread the weeks that I have duty, but after I get there, the dread disappears. Holy housework really makes me feel good inside. When I leave, I feel better about myself and about the world around me. Maybe it comes from 'hanging out' with the Lord for a while."

The sacristy should be a place of quiet serenity even in the midst of preparing for the most complicated of services. It is not a place to exchange gossip or to complain. Nor is it the place to compare the new rector with dear old Father Kazunkis and how he did things. Father Kazunkis is no longer there! And how he wanted things has nothing to do with anything. Strife has no place in the sacristy.

There is nowhere other than the sanctuary, that love, trust, charity, and mutual understanding should be more in evidence than in the sacristy. No one is perfect. Everyone, at one time or another, is bound to make a mistake. When, not if, but *when* that happens, the world will not come crashing down around your ears. The Lord will still be in his heaven. The Mass will still be valid. The priest will still love you. And you'll make very sure you never make that mistake again. (So will your team captain or altar guild director!)

One way to help create and maintain a good, loving, working relationship among guild members and between the altar guild and clergy is to keep lines of communication open. We need to talk about the hows, whos and whys of services, in a manner of good Christian fellowship and caring.

Make every new member of the group know that he or she is welcome and that their ministry is important not only to the church, but to you as well. See to it that new members learn the various aspects of the work so well that they feel comfortable in doing it.

CONCLUSION

A good way to keep lines of communication open is to have regular altar guild meetings to discuss changes in routine, deal with any problems which may arise, and get to know one another better. Any meeting should begin or end with a special celebration of the Eucharist or prayer for the work and ministry of the altar guild.

All altar guild members should be formally received into their ministry at a parish Eucharist using the form for Commissioning Altar Guild Members and Sacristans found in the Book of Occasional Services, pages 165-166 (or pp. 180-181, if you have the 2nd edition).

Begin and end your work with prayer. Our prayer for you is joy and a growing sense of the love of God in your work at His Altar.

"May the words of my mouth and the work of my hands be always acceptable in your sight, O Lord, my strength and my redeemer."

Amen.

GLOSSARY OF TERMS

Academic Hood

Worn to signify a college degree, usually the highest one possesses. It may be worn during choir offices over cassock and surplice. The shape, size and colors denote the type of degree, and the granting college institution or university.

Advent

Begins the fourth Sunday before Christmas Day, and the Sunday on or nearest Saint Andrew's Day, November 30, and ends with Midnight Mass on Christmas Eve, December 24.

Aisle(s)

The walkway(s) between sections of pews in the Nave, or between a section of pews and the side walls. Used in various liturgical activities (i.e., Stations of the Cross, the Great Litany, processions, etc.)

Alb

A long, full white garment. It may be worn over a cassock or alone.

Alms Basins

Also known as "offering plates." Often brass or silverplate containers used for the collection of alms.

Altar

From the Low Latin word *altar, altare*. The table that is center of our worship, the focal point of the eucharistic celebration. Located at the east-end of the church building, some altars may be attached to the wall. More recently, however, they are freestanding.

Altar Book

Contains the service of the Eucharist in all its variations. It also contains the music for conducting a sung Eucharist. It is also called the *Missal.*

Altar Cross	A cross used either on, behind or above an altar. Usually without decoration, it may also be a Crucifix or a Christus Rex.
Altar of Repose	An altar set up away from the sanctuary following the Maundy Thursday stripping of the Altar.
Amice	A rectangular neckpiece or collar, sometimes worn with an alb to protect the alb from soiling.
Antependia	Also called *pulpit falls* and *lectern falls*. Decorative material, usually in seasonal colors, that hang over the front of the pulpit or lectern (or both).
Ascension	The Thursday forty days after Easter celebrating Christ's ascension into heaven. It is a major feast and is commemorated only on the day itself.
Ash Wednesday	Marks the beginning of the Lenten Season. The day takes its name from the ceremony of the imposition of ashes on the foreheads of the faithful with the words, "Remember that you are dust, and to dust you shall return."
Aumbry	Essentially a 'wall safe' that is designed to contain the Reserved Sacrament, usually set into the wall on the gospel side of the sanctuary. A second aumbry may be located in the sacristy to contain the *oleum infirmorium* (oils for the sick) and *chrism*, used in baptism.
Baldaccino	Pronounced "bald-a-keno," hangings that are suspended from columns surrounding an altar.

Banners	Decorative materials that are hung from the ceiling or walls, or carried in procession, as with an official banner for the parish. Seasonal banners and banners for special occasions add color and excitement to worship.
Baptism	One of the two Dominical Sacraments. The sacrament of initiation into the Church, the Body of Christ.
Baptism (appropriate time for)	The most appropriate times for baptism are The Feast of the Baptism of our Lord (the first Sunday of Epiphany), the Easter Vigil, Pentecost, and All Saints'. However, baptism can be done during any service of the church at any time.
Baptismal Font	Usually located just inside the nave after entering from the narthex, the font (from the Latin word *fons,* meaning 'fountain') is the church furnishing that holds the holy water for the sacrament of baptism. Often made of stone or ornately carved wood, fonts come in a variety of sizes and shapes.
Bible Markers	Wide ribbons in the color of the day used to mark the Bible citations or Proper for the day.
Bier Lights	Tall candlesticks which stand on the nave floor beside a coffin during the Burial Office. There may be two, four, or six of them, used in pairs.
Bishop's Candle	A single candle which may be placed on the altar in addition to the eucharistic lights when the bishop celebrates the Eucharist.

Bishop's Chair	A dignified chair placed on the gospel side of the sanctuary when the bishop is present.
Bishop's Choir Dress	Vestments worn by a bishop as badges of the episcopal power and office. Cassocks and other wardrobe worn by a bishop are usually magenta or blue violet, or black with magenta piping and buttons.
Bread Box	A small, chambered box, containing extra wafers.
Burial Office	The Liturgy for the Burial of the Dead is essentially an Easter Mass of the Resurrection. There is also a Burial Office when there is to be no Requiem Mass.
Burse	A case placed on top of the veiled communion vessels to hold the corporal and extra purificators. It matches the chalice veil.
Candelabra	Lights (usually seven-branch candlesticks) used for special occassions such as Christmas, Pentecost, Easter and weddings. They are generally placed behind the altar on the gradine or near the altar.
Canopies	Hangings suspended from the ceiling or back wall and extending over the altar and footpace. Also called *testers*.
Cassock	The basic dress of clergy, choir, and lay assistants. It is a long, skirted garment which reaches from shoulder to ankle, usually black, but varying according to the rank and duties of the wearer.

Censer	A vessel in which incense is burned on charcoal. It may be carried in processions, used to cense the altar and the Gospel Book at the time of the reading of the Gospel, and the altar during the consecration. Also called a *thurible.*
Cerecloth	A waxed linen the exact size of the altar slab, designed to protect the fair linen from the dampness of stone altars, or the stains from wooden ones.
Chalice	A cup which is used at the altar to hold the elements of wine and water for consecration and communion.
Chancel	The area of the church building that is immediately in front of and slightly raised above the nave, containing the pulpit, the lectern, the choir, and the sanctuary.
Chasuble	A type of ecclesiastical coat worn by the celebrant during the Mass, from the Offertory through communion.
Chimere	A long black or magenta sleeveless coat-type gown worn by a bishop, that is open down the front.
Choir Dress	See *choir vestments*.
Choir Vestments	A term used to describe the garments worn at all services other than celebrations of the Eucharist. (Also called *choir dress.*)
Christmas	Begins with the first Mass on Christmas Eve, December 24, and continues through twelve days of Christmas until the Feast of the Epiphany, January 6.

Ciborium	Container that resembles the chalice, except that it has a lid. It is used to contain the bread (wafers) at the Eucharist.
Cincture	A wide, cumberbund-like garment that is worn around the waist with two strips of material that hang from the top of the waistband. The color or piping of the cincture matches the cassock. Sometimes called a *girdle*.
Co-adjutor Bishop	A bishop who automatically becomes diocesan bishop on the retirement, resignation, or death of the diocesan bishop.
Cope	A choir vestment of dignity which may be worn by any order of the clergy. It is a long semicircular cloak of rich material generally matching other vestments in the color of the season.
Cotta	Usually worn by acolytes, a *cotta* is the same as a surplice, but shorter. Whereas clergy surplices may be adorned by an embroidered cross, cottas are plain.
Choir	From the Greek word *khoros,* meaning 'a dance ring,' the choir refers to either the singers who provide music for a service or the place where they are located in the church building.
Chrism	Holy oil used in baptism.
Christus Patiens	Referring to the Suffering Christ, a crucifix that may be used as an altar cross.
Christus Rex	Usually referring to an altar cross of Christ the King, in royal robes and golden crown.

Confession   See *Reconciliation of a Penitent.*

Confirmation   One of the minor sacraments. A liturgy
                                    of 'confirming' a person in the faith and
                                    to a ministry within the Body of Christ.
                                    Usually performed when the bishop is
                                    making a parish visitation.

Corporal   A ninefold placemat designed to protect
                                    the fair linen and to catch any conse-
                                    crated particles or drops of wine which
                                    might fall on it during the Eucharist.

Credence Table   Originally a small side altar, it is a small
                                    table or shelf usually at the epistle side
                                    of the altar. On it are placed the things
                                    used for the celebration of the Eucha-
                                    rist which are not, at first (if ever)
                                    placed directly on the altar. Sometimes
                                    a credence table is used also in the
                                    nave to hold the elements that are
                                    brought forward during the offertory.

Crosier   The shepherd's crook carried by or in
                                    front of a bishop in his or her own
                                    diocese. It is a symbol that the bishop
                                    is a shepherd to Christ's flock. Also
                                    called the *pastoral staff*.

Crucifix   Referring to the Suffering Christ, or
                                    Christus Patiens, that may be used as
                                    an altar cross.

Cruets   Containers that are usually made of
                                    glass (or crystal), and used to contain
                                    the water and wine during celebration
                                    of the Eucharist.

Dalmatic   A type of ecclesiastical coat, worn by
                                    the deacon during a Solemn High
                                    Mass.

Deacon's Stole	A stole worn over the left shoulder, with the ends either looped or tied on the right side, just below the cincture. Worn as a badge of ordination by a deacon.
Diocesan Bishop	The highest ecclesiastical authority in a diocese. Elected and consecrated for life.
Dominical Sacraments	Of the seven sacraments, the two sacraments specifically instituted and commanded by our Lord, namely Holy Baptism and Holy Communion.
Dossal	A long heavy curtain, usually in old gold, deep burgundy, or green, that covers the area that would be taken by a reredos.
Easter	The day that the church celebrates the resurrection of our Lord from the dead.
Epiphany	Season that begins on the twelfth day of Christmas, January 6, also known as "Twelfth Night." It is the season which commemorates the manifestation or "showing forth" of Christ to the Gentiles. The last day of Epiphany is Shrove Tuesday, before Ash Wednesday.
Episcopal Ring	The symbol of the bishop's authority, usually worn on the third finger of the right hand.
Eucharist	One of the two Dominical Sacraments. The central act of worship in the church. Also known as *Holy Communion* and *The Lord's Supper.*
Eucharistic Candles	See *Eucharistic Lights*.

Eucharistic Lights Two candles that are placed on the altar during celebration of the Eucharist. Also called *eucharistic candles.*

Eucharistic Vestments Refers to vestments related to the celebration of the Holy Eucharist.

Ewers Vase-shaped pitchers that are commonly made of pewter or silver, and are used to contain the water and wine during celebration of the Eucharist. Frequently, a ewer is used to hold the water for a baptism prior to its being blessed and poured into the font.

Fair Linen The linen on top of the altar, covering the entire top of the altar and hanging down over the ends to any length, even to the footpace.

Family Mass Usually a sung Eucharist (either Rite I or Rite II), with music and a sermon. For churches that have three "levels" of masses each Sunday, this is usually the service that is either before, after, or during Sunday School, and the one in which the children from Sunday School participate in some form.

Flagons Larger than cruets, frequently made of silver or pewter, flagons are used to contain the water and wine during celebration of the Eucharist.

Footpace See *Predella.*

Frontal From the Latin *frontalia,* an altar covering that is a floor-length hanging, the length of the altar, usually the color of the day or the season.

Frontlet

Also called a *superfrontal*, a narrow strip of the same fabric and design of the frontal which hangs from an under-cloth of the altar (to cover the connections used to support the frontal). However, a frontlet may be used alone to identify the seasonal or day color even if no frontal is used.

Funeral Pall

The covering placed over the casket when the body is brought into the church for service of Christian burial.

Girdle

A belt made of rope, worn at the waist over an alb.

Good Friday

The commemoration of the day of crucifixion of Our Lord. It is a day of deepest mourning marked with special services and observances. The Mass of the Presanctified may be observed, with Holy Communion administered from the Reserved Sacrament, since there should be no Sacrament present in the church from Good Friday until the Mass of the Easter Vigil when the supply is replenished. The crosses are usually veiled in black or dark red and the tabernacle door is left open. The processions are silent.

Gradine

A narrow shelf behind the altar against the wall. Originally part of the reredos, it holds the tabernacle, office lights, and, in some cases, flowers. Also called a *retable.*

Great Fifty Days

The period from Easter to Pentecost.

Great Vigil of Easter

Marks the beginning of the Easter season, usually held on Saturday night before Easter Sunday. The liturgy includes lighting the "new fire" and the paschal candle and frequently includes baptisms.

Holy Communion

See *Eucharist*.

Holy Matrimony

One of the minor sacraments of the church. Liturgy may, or may not, include a *Nuptial Mass*.

Holy Saturday

No Eucharist is celebrated on Holy Saturday. The liturgy is one of quiet hope and anticipation.

Holy Week

The final week of Lent, begins on Palm Sunday, and extends to the Eucharist concluding the Easter Vigil. Holy Week is the liturgical reenactment of the events in the last week of the earthly life of our Lord.

Host

A term used when referring to eucharistic bread after it is consecrated.

Humeral Veil

A large, wide scarf worn around the priest's shoulders and down both arms (and hands), as a protective veil in carrying the Blessed Sacrament from one place to another inside the church. It is used at Solemn Benediction of the Blessed Sacrament and sometimes in the procession to the Altar of Repose on Maundy Thursday.

Incense Boat

A separate container for incense used in various liturgies. It contains a spoon for spooning small lumps of incense into the thurible.

Jacobean Frontal

A *jacobean* frontal is usually heavy and completely covers a freestanding altar, hanging to the floor like a huge tablecloth, with fullness at its corners.

Last Rites	See *Unction.*
Laudian Frontal	A *laudian* frontal hangs like a jacobean frontal, except it is fitted at the corners.
Lavabo Towel	A small towel that is folded and placed across the lavabo bowl to be used when the celebrant washes his or her fingers during the offertory.
Lectern	Standing in the nave, the lectern (from the Latin *lectrum,* for a 'reading desk') is in the front and to our right, as we face the altar. It is the reading desk where the Old Testament, Psalm and Epistle are read. You may hear this referred to as the "epistle side."
Lectern Falls	Also called *antependia*. Decorative material, usually in seasonal colors, that hang over the front of lectern.
Lent	A season comprised of the forty days before Easter, not counting the Sundays, marked by solemn pentence and fasting.
Linen	A general term used to describe the various cloths used in liturgical services, i.e., *fair linens, corporals, purificators, lavabo* or *baptismal towels.*
Liturgical Space	The inside of the church that is used for some act of public worship.
Low Mass	The term usually refers to a Eucharist without music and with a minimal number (or no) servers.
Maniple	An ecclesiastical napkin worn over the arm.

Maundy Thursday	A celebration of the institution of the Holy Eucharist, held on Thursday of Holy Week, usually followed by the ceremonial stripping of the altar and sanctuary.
Mensa	The top of the altar, often marked with five crosses, one in each corner and one in the center, symbolizing the five wounds in the body of Our Lord.
Minor Sacraments	Of the seven sacraments, the five lesser or minor sacraments that are available to all, are Holy Confirmation, Holy Matrimony, Holy Orders, Penance, and Holy Unction.
Missal	See *Altar Book.*
Mitre	The official "hat" of the bishop, worn whenever performing an episcopal act. It is worn when in procession, at confirmations, ordinations, and whengiving a blessing. Its shape is symbolic of the tongues of fire which rested on the heads of the apostles on the day of Pentecost.
Monstrance	Usually of gold and/or silver, in a cruciform shape with a clear glass (or crystal), circular receptacle at its center (from which sunlight appears to radiate), the monstrance is designed to hold a consecrated Host that is exposed for adoration.
Narthex	The entry hall, porch or vestibule of a church. The word narthex comes from the Greek *narthex*, meaning 'a large fennel,' (a tall herb).

Nave	The nave (from the Latin word *navis,* meaning 'ship'), is the largest part of the central worship area of the church.
Nuptual Mass	Celebration of Holy Eucharist during the liturgy of Holy Matrimony.
Office Lights	Candles of medium height which may be placed either on a gradine or retable (usually three to a side) or beside the altar. The office lights are there (whether lighted or not) to indicate that the Sacrament is reserved. Although they do not have to be lighted for the Eucharist, they may be.
Oleum Infirmorium	"Oils for the sick," holy oils used for anointing those who are ill.
Ordo Calendar	A calendar designed to include the appropriate seasonal color and indicate major and minor feast days.
Outer Stole	A stole that is worn over, rather than under, the chasuble. It is usually of a wider design. Also called an *Over Stole.*
Over Stole	See *Outer Stole.*
Pall	A stiffened corporal placed over the chalice.
Paschal Candle	Lighted at the Easter Vigil, it stands in the sanctuary until Pentecost. Then it may stand by the font to be used at baptisms, or placed in the sanctuary at a Requiem Mass.
Pastoral Staff	See *crosier.*
Paten	A plate made of silver, gold, or ceramic to match the chalice. Upon it is placed

	the priest's wafer when the chalice is vested for Eucharist.
Pavement Lights	Any large pair of candles standing on the floor of the sanctuary.
Pew	Usually permanent church seating in the nave, facing the altar.
Pectoral Cross	A large cross, usually of precious metal worn around the neck and upon the chest.
Pentecost	Commemorates the descent of the Holy Spirit. Also called *Whitsunday*. Also refers to the season of Pentecost, which is from Pentecost Sunday to the beginning of Advent.
Piscina	Earlier, a piscina was a built-in stone basin in a wall near the altar, used by the celebrant during Mass for ablutions and to clean the vessels after Mass. More commonly today, a piscina (from the Latin word *piscina,* meaning a 'fish pond') is a stainless-steel sink in the sacristy with a drain directly to the ground. It is used to clean all vessels and linen that have held consecrated elements.
Prayer Desk	A kneeling desk from which the Litany is read. Most commonly it is placed in front of the sedilia for the celebrant's use. When used for the Litany its place is on the floor of the nave at the chancel steps.
Preaching Stole	A shorter, matching stole that is worn by the preacher in delivering the sacrament of the Word, while not functioning in the Eucharist, or if the preacher is also assisting with communicating the

faithful at the Mass. It is worn over a cassock and surplice, cassock-alb, or alb.

Predella

The raised area on which the altar stands (also called the *footpace.*) The word *predella* is an Italian word meaning 'footstool' or 'kneeling stool.'

Prie-dieu

A kneeler with an angled shelf (for holding books, etc.), frequently located in front of the sedilia, the choir, or a shrine.

Processional Cross

A cross of some beauty and importance affixed to a staff and carried high, usually but not always preceded or flanked by torch bearers. It leads the procession into the church. It may also lead gospel and offertory processions, as well as retiring processions at the end of Mass.

Pulpit

Usually, standing in the nave, the pulpit (from the Latin *pulpitum,* meaning 'platform'), is in the front and to our left. It is the place from which the Gospel is preached; therefore, this is often referred to as the "gospel side."

Pulpit Falls

Also called *antependia*. Decorative material, usually in seasonal colors, that hang over the front of the pulpit.

Purificator

A napkin-like cloth, designed to cleanse or wipe the lip of the chalice after each person is communicated.

Pyx

Sometimes in the shape of a dove or flame hanging near the altar, a pyx is used for reservation of the Blessed Sacrament. Today, most commonly the term refers to a container about the size of a pocketwatch, that is used to take consecrated hosts to the sick or shut-in.

Real Presence

The theological term that the church has given to the everyday elements of bread and wine, that, once consecrated, become the Body and Blood of our Lord.

Reconciliation of a Penitent

Frequently called *confession.* The Anglican position, as stated in the 1549 Prayer Book, is that those who can not quiet their consciences through private prayer are to confess to a priest, but shouldn't be offended if others do not. One confesses sin in order to be forgiven, not so that one may be punished.

Requiem Mass

The Liturgy for the Burial of the Dead. Essentially an Easter Mass of the Resurrection.

Reredos

A tall screen of wood or stone, usually carved with figures of the holy family, various Christian symbols, or saints, that stands behind the altar.

Retable

See *Gradine.*

Riddels

Tall curtains, usually matching the dossal, which enclose the altar at either end to furnish protection from drafts.

Rochet

A long, full-length surplice-type garment worn by a bishop, with full sleeves gathered at the wrist and worn under a chimere. Or, a rochet may be of plain sleeves worn over a cassock, without chimere.

Sacrament	An outward and visible sign of the inward and invisible Presence of Christ. There are seven sacraments in the Episcopal church: The two Dominical Sacraments, specifically instituted and commanded by our Lord, namely Holy Baptism and Holy Communion, and the five lesser or minor sacraments that are available to all, namely Holy Confirmation, Holy Matrimony, Holy Orders, Penance and Holy Unction.
Sacristy	A room (or series of rooms), usually adjoining the sanctuary, where the vestments, vessels, and other supplies necessary for the services are kept. The sacristy (from the Latin word *sacer,* meaning 'holy') is the non-observed liturgical space where the members of the altar guild do most of their preparatory and clean-up work. It is also the area where priests and servers gather and prepare for services.
Sanctuary	The part of the church beyond the altar rail is called the sanctuary, from the Latin word *sanctus,* meaning 'holy.'
Sanctuary Lamp	A candle that hangs near the aumbry or tabernacle and is kept ever-burning to mark the presence of the Reserved Sacrament.
Sanctus Bell	Made of brass or silver, and used most commonly at the Sanctus *(Holy, Holy, Holy Lord)* in the Mass, at the elevation of the elements, and to summon the people to make their communion. Also called a *sanctus gong.*
Seasons	Advent, Christmas, Epiphany, Lent, Easter, and the season after Pentecost.

Second Linen

Another linen that lays on top of a cerecloth, made the exact length and width of the altar, to which superfrontals are sometimes attached.

Sedilia

The frequently backless bench on the epistle side of the chancel (or the sanctuary) for the officiating ministers.

Shrine

A niche or side altar, usually in a cruciform church, set aside to honor a saint. A shrine may, or may not, include a candlerack.

Shrove Tuesday

So called from the ancient custom of going to the priest to be shriven (stripped) of one's sins by making confession and receiving absolution before beginning Lent the next day, Ash Wednesday.

Side Altar

An altar on either side of the main altar, or along the sides of the nave in large churches or cathedrals.

Solemn High Mass

A sung Eucharist with incense, sanctus bells, etc. It can be done using either Rite I or Rite II. The music can be anything from Gregorian Chant to guitars and drums. The celebrant may celebrate facing the congregation or the east wall.

Stations of the Cross

The fourteen stations of the cross are intended to represent by art or procession the progression of Christ from the Judgment Hall to Calvary. Also known as the *Via Calvaris* and the *Via Crucis.*

Stole

A long strip of cloth symbolizing and signifying the yoke of Christ, worn over the alb. It is the distinctive mark of a bishop, priest, or deacon.

Suffragan Bishop	A bishop who does not automatically become diocesan bishop on the retirement, resignation, or death of the diocesan bishop.
Sung Mass	Usually implies a Eucharist (either Rite I or Rite II), with music and a sermon.
Superfrontal	See *frontlet*.
Surplice	A long, loose-sleeved garment made of white, lightweight material, worn over a cassock. It may vary in length anywhere from fingertip to almost ankle length.
Tabernacle	Designed to contain the Reserved Sacrament, it sits on the retable (or gradine) behind the altar. It is lined with white linen and is often vested to match the altar hangings.
Testers	See *canopies.*
Thurible	See *censer.*
Tippet	A wide black scarf sometimes worn over a surplice for the choir offices.
Torches	Candle holders that are affixed to a staff. They come in pairs. There may be two, four, or six torchbearers for a service.
Tunicle	A type of ecclesiastical coat, worn by the subdeacon during a Solemn High Mass.
Unction	One of the minor sacraments, mistakenly called *'Last Rites.'* Available to anyone who is ill physically, emotionally or spiritually at any time, not just at the time of death. The liturgy provides for

the laying on of hands, with or without anointing, communion from the Reserved Sacrament, or a private celebration of the Eucharist with the sick person.

Vestments A term used to refer to clothing worn by participants in services of the church. As a rule, they evolved from the everyday clothing of the middle class during the late Roman Empire, and the clergy continued to wear them after fashions changed.

Veil The veil matches the vestments worn by the celebrant and is a covering for the communion vessels.

Wafer A term used when referring to eucharistic bread before it is consecrated.

Wedding Cushions Cushions that are placed on the altar step for the use of brides and grooms when they kneel.

Whitsunday See *Pentecost*.